To Eugenia
Enjoy

10-11-19
DBMinter

Just One
More Night

Just One More Night

Dorothy Jean Minter

urlink
PRINT & MEDIA

1603 Capitol Ave., Suite 310 Cheyenne, Wyoming USA 82001
1-888-980-6523 | admin@urlinkpublishing.com

URLink Print and Media is committed to excellence in the publishing industry.

Published in the United States of America
ISBN 978-1-64367-284-7 (Paperback)
ISBN 978-1-64367-283-0 (Digital)
26.02.19

Just One More Night
Dorothy Jean Askew Minter

ACKNOWLEDGMENT

I would like to thank all of the ladies who took time out of their busy schedule to respond to my questionnaire. I hope you enjoy reading the book.

— Dorothy Minter

DEDICATION

This book is dedicated to the memory of my mother, whose love extends beyond the grave; who sacrifced beyond measure, so that I could get an education. Her name was Rhode Ethel Washington Askew.

It is also dedicated to the memory of my father, who died before his dream of building a new house was fulflled and before he could see me grow up. His name was Larkin Askew.

FOREWORD

This story is for all the women who have loved their men and have gone through many trials and tribulations to hang in there. If you are currently in a compromising relationship, this story is for you. If you are engaged to be married, take time to know him.

In order to do justice to this story, I must bare my soul to the world and share with you my innermost thoughts. I must relive the good, the bad and the ugly.

CHAPTER 1

The Beginning of the End

It is the day after my husband's funeral. The crowd is gone. My children have also said their goodbyes, after my reassuring them that I would be OK. The Cowboys have just lost their game to Philadelphia. Only the television in my bedroom is on. There are usually televisions on in the den and breakfast nook also.

All of a sudden, I realized that I was alone in the house. It was the first time in eight months that I had been alone in the house. My husband had been home from the hospital for eight months. I had set up his hospital bed in the large living room that we seldom used, except on special occasions.

I left my bedroom and started down the long hallway that led to the living room. I knew he wasn't there, but habit compelled me to go anyway. When I turned the corner into the living room, there, in place of the bed, was an array of green plants that friends had sent for the services.

And although there were only plants there, I could see him lying there in his hospital bed. I could see the array of caregivers who came each day to take care of him. When he was in a good mood and you asked him how he felt, he would say with a lopsided smile, "I feel with my hands." I remembered the long hours, days and months that I spent in his room, watching television or reading a book. I would look over at the bed where he was lying and many times he would be looking at me. If I moved around the room, his eyes would follow me. Some how, we both knew that we were on our last journey, although we never verbalized it. I would go to his bedside and tell him how much I loved him. Sometimes he would say, "I love you, too," and sometimes he would say, "I know it."

No matter where I went, I always called back to see how he was doing. One day when I was leaving, I went to his bedside and told him I was getting ready to leave. He looked at me and said," Every time I see you, you're getting ready to leave." I turned around and went back to the bed and reminded him that I always come back.

And so it was, from April 18, 2008, until December 3, 2008. During that time he had been seriously ill and on continuous care several times. One day he would be totally unresponsive and the next day he would be talking in complete sentences. The nurse had predicted his demise four times, but finally decided that he was unpredictable. In early June, when the Vitas Hospice Chaplain came to see Florence, he asked him what his goal was and he told him, "to get well." The Chaplain was so upset and wanted to tell him that he was going to die. I would not let him do that because I did not want to take away his hope. About a month before he died, I had a dream. I dreamed I went to his bedside and he looked up at me and said, "Dorothy Jean, I can't make it, I just can't make it." In my dream, my response was,"Every thing is going to be all right. I promise."

During those months, he spent two five-day periods in respid. He knew where he was going and why. He also knew when he would be coming back home.

As I stood there, gazing at the flowers that occupied the space where his bed had been for the last eight months, I realized that he was gone, that I would no longer be able to come into the room and sit or talk with him. I would no longer be able to watch his eyes follow me across the room. Whatever we had was only a memory. Our earthly journey together had ended. I went back into the den and sat down by the fireplace. I remembered that being his favorite chair and his favorite place to sit. He would sit there and poke the fire as needed.

He could build the biggest fires you have ever seen. The wood would sometimes reach up into the small part of the chimney. As

I sat there and watched the fire glow, I remembered. What did I remember? I remembered our whole life together, the good times and the bad times. This is the story that I would like to share with the world.

On December 22, 19 days after my husband passed away, a strange thing happened. My son went to work and added wood to the fireplace as he always did. I would always add more wood during the day. On this particular day, the ashes needed taking out, so I did not add any more wood because I was leaving the house and the fire needed to burn down so that my son could clean out the ashes when he came home from work. When I arrived home that afternoon, my son was already home from work and had a big fire going. I said, "I see you took the ashes out" He said, "No Mom, I thought you did." My granddaughter, who lived with me, was out of town. No one had access to the house except my son and me. What happened to the ashes that were piled up over the grate? Did our eyes deceive us? I would like to think that Florence's spirit came back and emptied the ashes so that our son, David, coming home after a long day of hard work, could just build a fire. Was this his way of telling us that he would always be with us in spirit? God only knows.

All I know is that he is always in my thoughts; no matter where I am or what I am doing, he is always with me. I have dreamed about him for the last three nights. Sometimes I wish I had passed before him. Then I would not have to deal with the loss. But he needed me to take care of him.

Today is Christmas Eve. It has been three weeks since my husband passed. I had not wanted to go back to the cemetery where he was buried, but this morning when I awoke, I knew this was the day. I called the cemetery office and asked them about their rules and regulations. She said the cemetery was open until four p.m.

I did not tell any of my family I was going, because I wanted to go alone and I was afraid if they knew, they would want to come with me.

I knew that he was buried in the Garden of Gethsemane, but I could not find the grave. Finally, I looked and saw the grave. It had fresh dirt and did not have a headstone.

As I approached the grave, I did not feel anything. I wondered why I felt this way. Had I not accepted the reality that he was gone? After all, this was the love of my life buried there. I was supposed to be remorseful and teary eyed, but I wasn't. Was it because the night before I had written about his first of many infidelities? I stood there for a moment and said, " Florence, this is Dorothy Jean. Thank you for emptying the ashes from the fireplace." Then, I immediately walked away, got in my car and drove back to the office to look at headstones. I kept thinking that I needed to go back and talk to him some more, but I didn't have anything else to say.

When I came home, my son and granddaughter were getting ready to leave for the evening. I was alone in the house. I began to think about Christmas Eve down through the years. Sometimes he was there and sometimes he wasn't. I refused to feel sorry for myself. As a matter of fact, I was glad to be alone in the house. I sat and watched television for a while and then went into the kitchen to prepare Christmas dinner for the next day. The next morning I awoke about seven a.m

. My first thought was that this was my first Christmas dinner without Florence. He would usually sit in his favorite chair in the den while I cooked. Every once in a while he would say, "What time is the bell gonna ring?" It seemed so strange that he was no longer with us in body. But he was certainly with us in spirit; not at the graveyard, but at home.

I now dream about him every night. Can you imagine dreaming about the love of your life every night and awaking to realize that he is not there...that it was only a dream. I keep thinking that every day my thoughts of him will begin to fade, but instead, they grow more intense.

I go to church and to the Senior Center and play dominoes. I go shopping, out to eat, read, watch television and many other activities, but no matter where I am or what I am doing, my thoughts are always of him.

Today is New Year's Eve. How time does fly. It has been four weeks since my husband passed away. Somehow, my mind keeps going back to the night of his death; the knock on the bedroom door and the nurse coming in to tell me that my husband had passed; quickly adding, "And he went peacefully."

I quickly went into the room and saw him lying there so still and he did look very peaceful. As I stood there gazing at his lifeless body, I thought about all of the things that he had gone through during the last two years. He spent almost a year in and out of nursing homes and hospitals.

How tired he must have been of the suctioning, the turning, the bathing and the long list of caregivers who invaded his privacy. It was like a free-for-all. Sometimes, he would play possum and not even talk to them.

I remembered last year's New Year's Eve. He had been home from the nursing home for two months. I stood by his bedside as the old year went out and the New Year came in. I talked to him about what was going on. We watched the television that was in his room. And now, another New Year's Eve was here and he was gone.

Down through the years we were almost always together on New Year's Eve, intimately or otherwise. And even though he is gone, the memories linger on.

Even if I went to church and he stayed home, which he usually did, I always left church so that we could be together to see the old year go out and the New Year come in. He would fire his gun in the air as we listened to gunshots all around us from other people in the community. So tonight I went to church. The night air was cold and brisk. I had put on extra clothing to make sure I did not get chilled.

It was a service of praise, thanksgiving and testimonies.

Several people got up and gave their personal testimonies.

The pastor preached a short sermon and breakfast was served after the benediction. I had no reason to rush home because Florence would not be there for us to ring in the New Year together.

I came home and went to bed, my mind engulfed with thoughts of him.

Oh, if I only had, "Just One More Night."

CHAPTER 2

Moving Day

Today is January 7, 2009. More than a month has now passed since my husband's death. I have asked his caregiver, Leon, to move all of his clothes out of his closet. I know this is something that needs to be done, but the finality of doing it just blows my mind. We have lived in this house for almost 24 years. It is going to be so strange to open the door to his closet and not see his clothes, always so neatly hung.

My plans are to move my winter clothes and all of my Sunday hats into his closet. Is that going to be a problem for me? I don't know.

Thinking about this brought to my mind my sister's death. Her daughter and I were disposing of her belongings I came across her eye drops and thought to myself, *She may need these,* so I put them aside. About that time reality hit and I realized how foolish that thought was.

So, how am I going to react tomorrow when we begin taking his clothes out of the closet? I looked in his closet earlier today. I went over every square inch of space: his shoes, his hats and caps, his pants and shirts and everything in his closet; but most of all, his overalls. He loved to wear his overalls.

He always kept such a neat closet, not at all like mine. He will probably raise up in his grave when I clutter up his closet.

I started going through his cancelled checks that he had saved in perfect order for many years.

Everywhere I go, everywhere I look: so many memories. How can I cope with all of these feelings?

I went to the garage to look for some tape. When I opened the drawer to the desk beside the chair where he sat, I saw one of his wind chimes. He loved to sit in the garage and watch them blow in the wind.

What else did he have in the garage? He had a microwave oven, two refrigerators, two televisions, a telephone, an easy chair and two extra chairs. Every day that the weather permitted, he sat in the garage watching television and the kids playing in the park across the street.

It was no big deal for him to go to the store and spend $40 or $50 on t-bone steaks. When I expressed my concerns about extravagant spending, he would look up at me and say (with a lopsided grin), "A hundred years from now, we won't know the difference.

He bought every kind of seasoning that you could ever need. He also liked to fish and hunt. He almost always had one or two bird dogs and he trained them himself.

Today is moving day. I awoke about five a.m. and remembered that the weather man had predicted beautiful weather, sunny with a high of 72 I opened the window shade by my bed so that I would be able to see the beautiful sunrise. It had been five weeks since my husband had passed.

There is such a calm in the air today. The roosters in the chicken yard did not crow this morning. I had planned to stay in bed until seven o'clock, but I could not rest in bed, so I got up at six a.m. I went to the kitchen to make coffee;

remembering that Leon was coming to help me with moving day. I made extra coffee, just as I had done all of those months when he came at seven to take care of my husband.

I then went outside to pick up the paper. It was a perfect day, one of those kind of days that Florence would get up early and go sit in the garage and watch the kids walk to school.

There is an elementary school next door to our property. As a matter of fact, we had sold some of our land to the school district for a school parking lot.

19

The beautiful weather reminded me of the day of his funeral. The weatherman had predicted cold weather with high winds, but it was a very nice day instead.

I came back inside and called Leon to tell him that I was up, the coffee was ready and that he could come on to work whenever he was ready. I left the garage door up as I always did when Leon was coming. Only this time, he was not coming to take care of "boss man," as he called him. He was coming to move the clothes out of his closet.

I sat down in the den with my coffee and waited for Leon. The news on the television was all about the death of actor John Travolta's son and the death of a police officer.

At that moment, I realized just how blessed I was. God had allowed us to be together almost 44 years, which was more than three times as long as Travolta's son had lived and a few years longer than the officer had lived.

When Leon arrived, he sat down and had a cup of coffee. He then began the arduous task of taking Florence's clothes out of the closet. The day was emotionally draining. I sat there for a while and watched Leon sort, fold and neatly pack his clothes in bags, so they could be stored in the shed outside.

Florence had built this shed about 20 years ago. It looks like a little house. He bricked it to match the house and put a window on each side. And now this shed was about to become the storage place for his clothes.

We found new pants, socks, shirts and gloves in his closet that had never been worn.

I found an excuse to go to the store and when I returned he had almost finished with Florence's clothes. He told me he had put some of his things in his bathroom cabinet. He said it as if he would be able to use it. When I looked in the bathroom, I saw a razor and some other items that Leon had placed on an open shelf over his sink. As a matter of fact, he took me into the bathroom to show me what he had done. He wanted me to see how he had arranged it. Poor Leon. Did he need a reality check? I just said," That looks nice,"and went on to finish the closet job.

After getting all of his clothes out of the closet, except for two jackets that I could wear, we began to move some of my clothes into his closet. I began to wonder if it may be too soon, but I had been most anxious to get this done. I had asked some of my friends who had lost their husbands and the time range was from two weeks to two years. One lady said her husband had been dead for eight years and his things were just as they were when he died.

CHAPTER 3

The Pity Party

Today I was thinking back to the day my husband passed until now. No matter how sorrowful I felt, I didn't cry much. The day he died, I hardly cried at all.

The next day when they called me to let me know that the body was ready for viewing, I went over and looked at the body. My heart was heavy, but I did not cry. I called some relatives to let them know that the body was ready for viewing. When they came and got ready to leave, I realized I did not want to leave. I just wanted to sit there with him. I started to cry and told my niece that I did not want to leave him. I soon stopped crying and everybody left. I sat there for a long time and finally went home, but I couldn't cry anymore. On the day of the funeral, I hardly cried at all. My eyes filled with tears, but I needed a good boo hoo "pity party."

The day after moving day I was moving some of my clothes into drawers that had previously been his. I had listened to a tape that my friend had given me with Bennie Hinn on faith, with many scriptures of encouragement. After that I played a tape that Florence and I had listened to over the last few months.

When one of our favorite songs from the tape started playing, memories flooded my soul. The song was one of Sam Cooks and it went something like this:"Lights turned way down low, music soft and slow. You know I love you so." That's where it's at, the "pity party " began. I cried and cried until I could not cry anymore. It really felt good. It was like a heavy weight had been lifted off my chest. I don't know how many more "pity parties" there will be, but I will not hold back if I feel the need to cry.

Today is Sunday, January 11, 2009. I went to Sunday school and church. The "pity party" is over for now. I came home from church and finished cooking dinner. After dinner, our youngest son, Rory, came to visit. We decided to go out to the cemetery and visit the grave. It was a good trip. I did not shed a tear. I just talked to him a little bit and it felt good. I told him I loved him and we were going to straighten up the flowers on his grave. Then Rory and I told him goodbye and left.

A few days later, his saving's account check came, and I divided it equally among the five children. They were happy and so was I. It was what he wanted, although it was not stipulated in the will.

I have not fully accepted the fact that he is gone. How I wish I could have "Just One More Night." My memories took me back to the 1960s. We had moved from a one-bedroom apartment to a two-bedroom house.

My mother had come to live with us after David was born and continued to live with us so that I could work and also go back to school to finish my degree. The two-bedroom house was small but better than the one-bedroom apartment. My mother shared the bedroom with the children and my husband and I shared the other bedroom.

This was the first house we had with an indoor toilet. Our first home, had an outhouse. While we were living there, we had a chance to buy a new house. While he was working on the house, he got a job at General Motors on the night shift. Every night when he came home, he would climb into bed and cuddle up behind me and we would sleep that way and wake up in the morning with his arms still wrapped around my waist. Oh how I wish I had "Just One More Night." Of course I know that this can never be, except in my dreams and always in my thoughts.

Today is January 23, 2009. We have a new President, Barack Obama. My husband had a chance to vote and lived to see him get the nomination, but passed away before the Inauguration. As I sat at home and watched the festivities, my eyes were on the television, but my thoughts were on him. How proud he would have been, just as most of us are, to see a black man become President of the United States.

Yesterday, I went to work. I thought this would help to distract me from thinking about Florence, but it didn't. Yesterday was not a good day. I had a "pity party" without tears. I felt sorry for myself. "Why did he have to die?" But I know that God knows best and that His will must be done; that he has paid a debt we all will have to pay one of these days. He can't come to me, but I can meet him in heaven.

Today is March 3, 2009. Florence has been dead three months. I knew this was the third of the month, but I never thought about it being the date he died until about seven in the evening. Is this a sign that I am getting better? This is the time of the year when he would begin getting his ground ready for planting. I looked out in the back yard and saw the garden plow. If he were alive and able, he would be plowing the ground and getting it ready for planting. The onions and greens would already be in the ground. My son is planting a garden, but it is not quite the same.

I continue to dream about him almost every night and, of course, I think about him every day. The fact that I will never see him again is overwhelming. I try to rewind the clock, but it just won't rewind. I try to rewind it for,"Just One More Night."

CHAPTER 4

The Basketball Game

It was a cool spring day. The trees had just begun to put on their spring beauty. The farmers were already planting their crops. I lived in the country and went to a little country school named Caney. My husband went to a little country school named Chapel, which was about two miles from my school.

It was basketball season and this was the day for the big game. My brother came to pick me up in a wagon to take me to the game. As we approached the Chapel School campus, I saw this skinny kid running across the school yard. I know it sounds strange, but at that moment, at the ripe old age of eight, I fell in love with him. And I've never stopped.

Several years passed before he even knew I existed. When their school burned and they had to attend school in our church, it was the happiest day of my life. The church was located across the road from my school and every day at recess, he would come over and play croquet. He was about 14 and I was 12. Several girls had a crush on him and he played them all. Except for playing croquet with me, he had no other interest. After all, the other girls had all blossomed into womanhood and I was still looking like a little girl.

The next year the schools were consolidated and we were all together. He was one grade ahead of me. I guess he was what you call "mannish." He loved hugging the girls. One day, while we were standing in line, he hugged me. That was the happiest day of my life.

At last I was more than a croquet player. At last, I felt I had a chance to develop a relationship.

But this was not to be. At the end of the 1947 school year, the school dropped the eleventh grade. We had never had a grade twelve.

He entered his senior year in high school at Fred Douglas High School in Denton, Texas, where he had gone to live with his sister.

In the meantime, I entered my junior year in high school at Douglas High School in Sulphur Springs. Texas. You need to understand that during the '40s and '50s, dating was quite different from the way it is today. He had two or three girlfriends at that point and I had two or three boyfriends. He had a girlfriend named Margaret. At Christmas time he came home for the holidays. At the church Christmas tree, he gave Margaret a gift, but he did not give me one.

Regardless of what happened, I continued to love him.

How crazy is that?

CHAPTER 5

My Childhood and Beyond

I was born on a farm in Hopkins County in East Texas. The midwives had already delivered me before the doctor arrived. My conception was a total surprise to my mother. She had been married to my Daddy for seven years and was 40 years old when I was born. My Daddy was 47. Each of them had been married and brought children into the marriage. With my birth it was mine, yours and ours. My Daddy had two daughters and one son and my Mother had three sons. At the time of by birth, my sibling's ages ranged from 11 to 21. Both Daddy and Mother were hard workers. Every year, my Daddy was going to make enough money to build us a new home. It never happened. He always had to borrow money to make the winter, after all the debts were paid.

My Daddy was really mean to my Mother. Many times we had to run away to a safe place to let him calm down. He was always good to me and spoiled me rotten, but I never remember him saying, "I love you," but he showed it in his actions. He would carry me to school in his arms, rather than let me walk. He would buy spam for my lunch, because I did not like to eat in the lunchroom. We had a 40-acre farm, which did not really yield enough for us to get ahead; and although we never had extra money, we always had food and clothing and a roof over our heads. We had cows and sold milk. We raised chickens and hogs that we had for food. We had a vegetable garden and fruit trees. My mother always canned food to last us through the winter.

She was also quite resourceful in other ways. She used the printed flour sacks to make clothes for us. She used the good part of worn out pants and cotton sacks to make quilts for us. Quilting was an art in those days. Women in the community would come together in the community and help each other quilt. After the harvest they had lots of time on their hands. Sometimes they would bring their children, but we had to stay in another room, because children, in those days, were not privy to adult's conversation. If you heard anything, you could never let them know you heard it. And from time to time, we did hear some things.

My Daddy and I went to Sunday school every Sunday morning and mother would come later to the eleven o'clock services. We also had Baptist Training Union on Sunday nights and had the Lord's Supper, once a month at night.

The unsaved could not sit on the same side of the church with the saved during sacrament. If they knew you had not joined the church and you did not move on your own, they would ask you to move to the other side of the church. I guess this was to make sure you were not accidentally given bread and wine.

The women of the church made the unleavened bread at home. The wine was grape juice. I was appointed secretary of the Sunday School at the ripe old age of 10. The winters were cold, but the schools never closed for bad weather.

The school year was geared to the harvest of crops. We would go to school six weeks in the summer or until the cotton was ready to pick. Then the schools would close so that we could go out and pick cotton for six or more weeks. Many families took their children out of school to chop cotton and pick strawberries in the spring, but my mother never allowed me to miss any school to work.

My daddy died when I was nine years old and left my Mother 63 cents, four cows, two horses and a 40-acre, sandy land farm.

After my Daddy died, my Mother and I continued to live in the house. This turned out to be a nightmare because my mother believed the house was haunted. She would wake me up in the middle of the night, get me out of bed and we would go over to my aunt's house to spent the remainder of the night. I could never understand why she was so afraid of dead people and believed in ghosts.

During my daddy's lifetime, as I mentioned earlier, He would always buy me spam for mother to fix for my lunch, because I did not like to eat vegetables and did not want to eat the lunches being served at school.

The next year after my daddy died, things changed. My dad passed away in June, so to make sure I got off on the right foot, My Mother informed that when school started she would no longer pack my lunch. I would either eat in the school lunch room or go hungry. And oh, by the way, she kept her word.

The next two years were really rocky. We continued to live in the same house and from time to time, her ghosts would come back and away we would go, in the middle of the night, to my aunt's house.

It wasn't just having to leave the house, but we had to cross a log, over a small body of water that we called a branch, to get to my aunt's house or go miles to get around it. I was not afraid of ghosts, but I was afraid to walk that log. The water was at least six feet deep. I could not swim and neither could my mother.

In the summer of 1944, my uncle had a rent house that had been vacated and my mother asked if we could rent it. He rented it to us and we moved into this two room house, which was located on the main country road. This was almost like moving from the country to the city. We saw people and cars coming by every day. The house we had lived in was located at the end of a cotton field about a mile off the road.

In the meantime, my mother was receiving a check from two of my brothers in the army. She also went to work as a cook for the school. By that time, I had already learned to eat vegetables, both at home and at school.

My uncle owned a lot of land. He owned 10 acres across the road from where we were living. My mother convinced my uncle, who was my Daddy's brother, to sell her the land. She took money she had saved from her army checks and bought the land. Then, she had a two-bedroom house built on the property. Can you believe it? During those days, it only took about $30 worth of materials to build the house. It had two bedrooms, a kitchen, front porch, and a screened in back porch that served as an extra sleeping area, when needed.

The talented and not so talented men did all of the work. We were so proud of that house. We could hardly wait to move in.

The house was imitation brick. My mother had no building costs. All she did was bring them food. That was not uncommon in those days. When anyone in the community needed help or had a project, the people in the community just volunteered their services.

My mother was quite resourceful. We had no water source, so we had to haul our water in barrels.

One day, my mother was walking down the road and about a hundred feet from the house she saw water running out of the ground. She was so excited. She came back to the house to tell me the good news. She dug it out and did whatever was necessary to capture the spring water. Yes, there was a spring, right there in the ditch by our property. It is quite likely that it came from under the ground on our property.

After my mother found water for us it made things a lot easier. We did not have to depend on other people to haul us drinking water. We would wash a few things at home, but had to take our big washing to a pool to wash them. There were washtubs and rub boards available at the pool.

When my brothers came home from the Army, they lived with us for a while. My baby brother got married and moved to Tyler, Texas. My oldest brother stayed with us until he got married and moved to town with his wife. He had bought a car at that time. One night he came home late and went to bed. We began to smell something and looked outside and his car was on fire. The flames were leaping at the house. The imitation brick was the only thing that saved the house. There was also some water in a barrel that he had hauled to the house. He used it to put out the fire.

After both my brothers got married and moved out, my mother and I continued to live in the house until I finished high school and went to college. As a matter of fact, we were still living there when I got married.

I graduated from high school at the age of sixteen, as valedictorian of my class and received a scholarship to Butler College in Tyler, Texas. My mother was such a remarkable and loving person. She always sacrificed for her family. I always picked cotton until time to go to school. My mother continued to pick cotton after I left for college that year. She picked as long as there was cotton to pick. The money was always sent to me if I needed it.

My first year in college was a good one. I lived in a dormitory and the rules were very strict. The students could not be off campus after six p.m. unless the school matron escorted you, or you were classified as a senior. How we envied those seniors who had all of those privileges.

We had to catch the city bus to get downtown, and yes, we had to sit on the back of the bus. And if all the seats were taken and a white person got on the bus, a black person was required to get up and give them their seat.

One day rings clearly in my mind. It was the last bus we could catch in order to get back to the campus before six p.m. It just so happened that on that day our science teacher, Coach Roberson, was on the bus coming back to campus. The bus quickly filled to capacity. All other passengers would have to stand. At the next stop, a white male got on the bus. The bus driver looked around for him a seat and saw that they were all filled. He then asked Coach Roberson to get up and give the white man his seat. I will never forget the look on Coach Roberson's face as he slowly got up and said, " I'm a man just like he is."

All of us as black people have experienced or witnessed similar situations. There was a time that when you went into a store to make a purchase, as long as white people were coming in, you had to wait until there were no more whites to be waited on before they would wait on you.

Living on a black college campus during those days had many challenges. On Sundays, we were only served two meals, breakfast and lunch. You were given a tiny sandwich at lunch to eat for your supper. There was a cafe across the street from our dormitory. The only problem was that, even if you were lucky enough to have some money, you could not go off campus on Sunday to buy food. Our only recourse was to go down to the fence and hope the owner would come out and see us. When he did, we would order over the fence and he would bring the orders back over the fence to us.

We did not have washers and dryers, but washed our clothes outside the dormitory, under a tree. We used a washboard and two tubs.

It was a big thing for the girls to wash and iron their boyfriend's shirts. I had a boyfriend named John, who wore white shirts most of the time. How I detested washing and ironing those shirts. I can assure you that relationship did not last very long.

Some of the students had parents with transportation and would get to go home for the weekends. My mother did not have transportation or the money to pay someone to pick me up . So I only came home for Thanksgiving, Christmas and Easter. It was only 60 sixty miles away, but it may as well have been 600 miles.

I had several boyfriends that year. Besides John, there was Calvin, who wanted to marry me, and two others, whose names I cannot remember for the life of me. And then there was my homeboy, Lloyd Ross, who was there attending Tyler Barber College.

I guess you are wondering where Florence was during that time. He was living and working in Denton but came home the next summer. I guess we had really drifted apart,.As a matter of fact, we had never had a close courtship. We also had a dorm lights curfew, which was twelve o'clock midnight. The dorm matron stayed off campus a lot trying to keep up with a much younger man she had married. So we would sometimes play cards way past midnight. We would hear her coming and turn the lights out and remain real quiet until she went away. We always took our books when we went to play cards. Then if we happened to get caught in the hall, we could always say we were studying. Now there is not a matron in the world who would not forgive you for studying after curfew.

And so it was, the fall turned into winter and the winter into spring, and before we knew it, the year was over and we all went home.

During that summer I stayed home with my mother. I had dated a homeboy that I really liked. In the meantime,

Florence came home for the summer. We went to a Fourth of July picnic. He was there with his girlfriend and I was there with my boyfriend.

After that we started seeing each other again. He did not want me to see other people and I did not want him to see other people. So for the remainder of the year, we only saw each other.

I did not get to go back to school in the fall because we did not have enough money. We found out that Bishop College was on a quarter system and the second quarter did not begin until December. My pastor's daughter, Mildred, was going there, and we made arrangements to room together off campus.

I enrolled in Bishop College in December of 1950. Living off campus meant that you were really your own boss. We lived two blocks from campus and had to walk to class, which was no problem at all. Just before school was out I met a guy who was a nephew to the lady I was renting a room from. When he tried to talk to me I told him OK as long as he understood that I had a boyfriend at home who was my true love.

I finished that year and went back the next fall for the 1951-52 school year. When I came home for Christmas, Florence was dating my cousin, so when I went back to school. "J" and I started going steady. I really did like him. He was attending Wiley College. During that spring semester I became pregnant with his child. My boyfriend led me to believe that he wanted to marry me. Before I became pregnant, he told me when we were at the movies one night that he wanted to marry me, and I told him that I liked him, but that Florence was the love of my life.

I knew that his mother was not in favor of him getting married. One day he picked me up from the college campus and drove me to Atlanta, Texas. He told me he had a surprise for me. I was wondering what the surprise might be. Was he going to marry me against his mother's wishes? I was going to have his baby while I was yet wondering as we approached a railroad track. He stopped and parked the car. Then he told me he had arranged for the lady who lived in that house across the tracks to perform an abortion. When I refused to get out of the car, he slapped me very hard across the face. He brought me back to campus. We never spoke a single word to each other all the way back to campus. He let me out and went on his way.

I felt that I had let my mother down. She had worked so hard and sacrificed so much for me to get an education and here I was pregnant. I only saw him one more time that school year. He came over to see his aunt.

When I came home for Easter, Florence and my cousin were no longer an item. I had strep throat while I was home for Easter and was very sick. Mother did not know that I was pregnant. I went back to school and did not tell anyone. When school was out and I came home, I was not showing. But after a few weeks I had to tell my mother. There is one thing about pregnancy, if you don't tell, it will eventually come to light.

Florence and I started dating again. At first, he did not know that I was pregnant. I just knew that when he found out that would be the end of our relationship. I was so wrong. He kept on dating me until the baby was born in November. She was such a beautiful baby. I could not imagine my life without her. I never had any regrets for keeping her.

After the first of the next year, he went back to Denton. It was the year of 1953. He only came home twice that year, once in February and again in December.

I was not able to go back to school. Mother kept the baby and I went to work at the laundry in Sulphur Springs. My mother never once scolded me for having the baby, she just loved us, even though I knew she had to be disappointed that I did not finish college.

It was in the spring of '54 that I heard that Florence was getting married and that his girlfriend was pregnant with his baby.

CHAPTER 6

His Childhood and Beyond

Florence was the youngest of seven children. He had three brothers and three sisters. His mother died when he was two years old. After her death, he went to live with his older sister, who was already married. While he was a small child, she died from childbirth. He later told me that he really loved his sister and that her death had a devastating effect on him.

He then went back to live with his father for the next few years. His dad loved him, but he was not the type of dad to express it to him in words. He had two other brothers who also lived with the dad. They both went into the army. Florence did not go because of a broken arm at eight years of age that was never reset.

His dad finally married again and Florence loved his stepmother and she loved him. He stayed with his dad and his sister who lived in town until he moved to Denton to live with another sister. After he finished high school he went to work for Texas Woman's University as kitchen help. Later he went to work for the University of North Texas and was working there when we married in 1955.

During this same period, I remained at home with my daughter and my mother. I was working at the laundry in town.

During that time, we dated other people, but we always got back together. He continued to live in Denton and I remained at home with my mother and daughter.

When he came home at Christmas we saw each other but he was not ready to make a commitment. I had dated other guys, but Florence was always my true love. I had heard that he was dating an older woman and also a younger girl who lived across the street from him.

He came home that year for Christmas. In the meantime, he became engaged to the girl who lived across the street from where he lived. They were to be married in June and this was the talk of the town.

I also found out that she was expecting a baby. I felt like I had lost him forever.

Spring and summer came and went and then it was fall. It was sometime during the fall that I found out that they did not get married. In November of 1954, a baby boy was born to his girlfriend. He was the spitting image of Florence.

CHAPTER 7

The Marriage

In December of 1954, one month after his son was born, he came home for the Christmas holidays. In the mean time, when I thought he had married, I was dating a soldier and we became engaged. He gave me a beautiful engagement ring. I found out later that he had broken an engagement with another girl to marry me.

When Florence came home at Christmas, we saw each other. We rode from the East End, (which was the hang out) to his sister's house, which was only a couple of blocks away. He told me he wanted to get back with me and that he was not going to marry his son's mother. I informed him that our courting days were over. I would marry him but I would never court him anymore. I think someone told him I was engaged to a soldier. I found out later that someone did tell him that I was engaged. He may have seen the ring on my finger.

To my surprise, he said he wanted to marry me. I was officially engaged to another man and wearing his ring. He told me he would have a weekend off in two weeks and we could go to Oklahoma and get married without telling any one. He was trying to avoid facing my mother, who did not like him anyway. She never thought he was marrying material. My condition for marrying him was that he had to go to my mother and in my presence, ask for my hand in marriage.

It was a few days later that he came to the house. When I saw who was at the door, my heart skipped a beat. Many questions ran through my mind. Is he really going to ask for my hand in marriage? Am I really going to marry the love of my life?

We had a wood-burning heater and a big fire was burning. Florence picked up the poker and nervously began banging on the heater. He told my mother he wanted to marry me. After much discussion, she told him he had her permission to marry me, but if he decided he didn't want me, to remember where he found me.

In the meantime, on February 5, 1955, my brother's wife killed him. His name was Bruce.

On February 7, 1955, a Justice of the Peace married us. "Till death do us part," was a part of our marriage vow.

We spent our first night of marriage at his sister's house. The next day he went back to Denton and I moved two weeks later. We moved into a one-bed room apartment. Our rent was $20 a month and we could hardly afford that.

Florence was working in the kitchen at one of the dormitories at North Texas State University. I got a job there also, but in a different kitchen. My daughter stayed with my mother the first month and then we moved her to Denton to live with us, which was where she belonged. He legally adopted her.

In April of that year I became pregnant. I worked as long as I could. During that summer, I went home to visit my mother. When I came back, I found out that he had brought a woman there and they had slept together in our bed. This was the beginning of his infidelities.

I left work at the college and went to work at a cafe. That was the worst experience I ever had. They fired me after three weeks. After that I went to work for a boarding house and worked three or four months.

The delivery man was having an affair with the cook and they would do a lot of making out in my presence. This made me very uncomfortable. They knew I would not tell anyone. And even though I was pregnant, the owner of the boarding house made passes at me.

During that summer, my husband continued to work at the college. Times were hard and we could barely make ends meet. Sometimes, after paying rent and utilities, we had to borrow money to buy groceries. We could also buy on credit at the two neighborhood stores, Ebron and Mahan.

Many times my husband would steal food from the college where he worked. I heard that this was common practice among the workers.

One day when I went to pick him up from work, he had a whole case of food hidden outside and he put it in the car. On the way home, he had a wreck. I had to let him drive back home and I rode in the back seat. The children were also with us. Someone made a left hand turn if front of him, they did not have the right of way.

It was the era of the flare-tailed skirt and I just happened to be wearing one. So when the police came, I put the case of food between my legs and spread the skirt over it. The policeman asked if every thing was alright and we told him yes. I have never been so afraid in all my life. I don't remember whether or not the policeman did an accident report or not. I do know that he left without a problem, got in his car and drove away.

Sometimes he would come out from work, get in the car and pull a chicken from under his shirt. Things were a little better while I was working, but I had to quit three months before my baby was born.

Let's not forget that his son, who was only three months old when we married, had to be taken care of.

My husband would buy a case of milk every month. As a matter of fact, one of the first things I did after we married was deliver a case of milk to his son. He also bought clothes for his son.

Our son was born the next year on January 4, 1956. He took me to the hospital and stayed there until after he was born, When he left, I was expecting him to come back that day, but he did not. I found out he and his sister had gone to see his son, who lived with his mother. He was 14 months old at the time.

As far as I know, there was never another romantic relationship between him and his son's mother. She had another baby who was a month younger than our son. When she was seven months pregnant, she wanted us to keep his son because of her pregnancy. When my husband asked me about it, I told him no. How dare he ask me to keep their baby when I was one month further along than she was. My husband's sister took the baby and kept him until after her baby was born.

During that same year, about three weeks before my baby was born, something unbelievable happened. My husband had gone somewhere with his brother-in-law. My friend, who lived next door, had three sisters. One had a boy friend who drove a red convertible. The lady across the street sold bootleg whiskey. On this particular day, my friend's sister and her boyfriend had come to visit. He came through the back yard and went across the street to buy whiskey; at least that's what I think happened.

About nine-thirty p.m. my husband and brother-in-law came home. Both had been drinking. We lived in a shotgun duplex, so it was a straight walk through. The back door was open and the wind was out of the west, which was the direction the duplex faced. When he opened the front door, the back door slammed shut. My husband wanted to know who was in there with me. I told him no one, but he did not believe me.

My husband then went out the back door, onto the back porch. I wasn't worried because I knew no one had been here. My husband looked under the back porch and the young man who was dating my friend's sister, was hiding under the back porch.

Can You imagine how I felt, being totally innocent and not being able to prove it. I never talked with the boy to find out why he was there, and I don't think my husband did either. He had made up his mind that I was guilty and that was that.

The next day, I thought everything was over. My husband left the house and came back about four in the afternoon. He decided to make me tell the truth about what had happened the night before. So he threw me down on the bed, ripped off my maternity top. He then pulled his loaded gun out of the closet and pointed it at my head. I ran out of the house and started across the street and fell. The lady bootlegger saw me and came and helped me get up and back into the house. My husband had put the gun away and calmed down.

When our son was born, my mother came to stay with me during my recovery and my husband asked her to stay on so that I could work.

I began working at the laundry after my baby was a few weeks old. My mother continued to stay. In less than three months I was pregnant again. I continued to work at the laundry until 19 days before my baby was born.

Our second son was born that same year on December 26, 1956. After he was born, I went to work for a different laundry. The laundry where I was working had hired someone in my place for 10 cents an hour less than I was making. I was making 60 cents an hour.

I would get up early in the morning and go looking for work. One morning I went to Conn's Laundromat at about seven forty-five in the morning. It just so happened that his shirt presser did not show up for work that day. He hired me for 75 cents an hour. I was so thrilled and so was my husband. I worked there until the next summer. In the meantime North Texas State University had integrated and I wanted to go back to school to complete my degree. When I first told him that I wanted to go back to school, he was against it. It just so happened that I would be attending the same college where he was employed as a kitchen worker. Some of his so-called friends teased him and told him if I finished my education, I would leave him. He would come home and tell me what they said. I guess that is why he was so against me going back to school.

I was working at the laundry when I decided I was going back to school. When I first told him I wanted to go back to school, he told me if I did I would need to take the three children with me and get out. I informed him that I planned to finish college, with or without him, and that I would be gone when he came home from work.

The laundry where I worked was only two blocks from the college. He took me to work that morning and went on to his job. That afternoon about two, he came to my job. He told me that if I would stay and not leave, he would help me get in school, even if he had to borrow the money My reply to him was, "If you are going to help me, I'll stay, but if you're not, I'm gone." And so it was, from that time on, he supported me.

He was able to get the money for one summer session that year. I was so excited about going back to school. For the first two years, I could only afford to go in the summer. So the following fall, after the first summer session, I went to work for a nursery school.

After making passing grades for two summers, I was able to apply for a National Defense Student Loan. The loan paid for my tuition and books and I had a little left for my personal use.

After I started to college full time, I had to quit my job at the nursery. I got a job cleaning doctor's offices at night.

Florence was no longer at the college, but on construction. He would come home from work and go with me to help me on my job. My mother was still living with us, so she took care of the children.

As I look back on this time in our lives, I realize that these were probably some of the best years of our lives.

I graduated from North Texas State University in August, 1961. I was pregnant with my fourth child and did not get to teach that year. I began substitute teaching after my baby was born. I began my teaching career in the fall of 1962.

In 1964, we bought two lots and had a four-bed room house built on one of the lots. The other lot became a playground for the neighborhood, basketball goal included. My mother had a room, my daughter had a room, The three boys shared a room and my husband and I had a room.

This was such a happy time. I was teaching and my husband had been hired by General Motors Parts Division in Dallas. He was so proud to say, "I work for GM."

My husband loved to go to the country to share private moments with me. I wasn't that excited about it, but I knew our privacy was somewhat compromised at home, especially with my mother living with us.

My mother passed in 1967, and I was surprised that he continued to want to go to go the country for us to share our intimate moments. I knew he had a roving eye, but he had never been in a relationship that I was aware of. Except, of course, the one-night stand he had the same year we got married.

It was the summer of 1968. I decided to have a party and invite a few friends. Florence invited his friends and I did likewise. I invited one of my teacher friends that he had never met. As the night progressed, I noticed that they were spending a great deal of time together in low conversation.

After a while my friend said she had to go home. Her husband and children had gone out of town for the weekend and that is why I invited her to the party. She was the new teacher in town and had few friends.

A few minutes after she left, my husband said he needed to go to the store. Somehow, I knew he was lying. She had told me where she lived and her apartment number.

When he was not back in a reasonable length of time, I asked a friend to take me over to the apartments. No one knows how much I wanted to be wrong about him. How could my friend and my husband do this to me?

When we pulled up to the apartments, there was his truck in the parking lot. I got out of my car and went and knocked on the door. I could hear a hustle and bustle inside, but no one said anything. I called out and no one answered.

Then I noticed there was a window beside the door close to the ground so I entered through the window. Florence had hid in the closet and she was standing in the middle of the floor with nothing on but her bra and panties. I'll leave it to your imagination as to what happened next. When we left the apartment, my friend drove her car back and I rode with Florence. All he could say was, " I may as well get my clothes because I know you are going to put me out."

Of course I forgave him and told him he did not have to leave. After all it was " Till death do us part." No matter what he did, I could not imagine my life without him.

Florence always worked hard to take care of the physical needs of his family: food, clothing and shelter. He worked at GM and did odd jobs on the side. While working on construction as a brick tender, he had learned to lay brick, tape and bed sheetrock and do carpenter work as well. So he did small jobs laying brick or doing sheetrock or small carpenter jobs. He could also fix electric appliances. Although he did not have a college degree, he was a very smart man.

In 1970 I was appointed Director of Special Education. My husband was proud, but wondered what he could do to make more money than me. At that time, he was making more money at GM than I was teaching; plus he did odd jobs. But the director position gave me a $2,500 raise, which made my earnings a little bit more than his. I told him it did not matter, It was all ours.

After I became Director of Special Education, I was gone out of town a lot to meetings and conferences. He took a lot of responsibility for taking care of the children. Their ages were, eight, 13, 14 and 18.

For the next seven years, (1970- 1977) things were really good, or so I thought.

CHAPTER 8

The Anniversary Letter

Dear Florence,

I guess you thought I would never write. I have been so busy since you went away. David and Carlyon are still living here. Carlyon is in her second semester in college. She made all As last semester. She has changed her ma}or from teaching to nursing. She was so impressed with the nurses who came to see you that it inspired her to want to be a nurse. And of course, you know she helped David and me take care of you. David is keeping plenty of wood for the fireplace. You should see the back pasture. There is enough wood to supply Denton (smile).

Leon, your caregiver, is doing OK. He is working at the Grove's Ray of Hope that our church has established for recovering drug addicts.

Today is February 2. Tomorrow will mark the three-month anniversary of your passing. I want you to know that I think about you all the time.

I have only been to see you twice since you passed away. I guess you wondered why I did not have much to say and why I stayed such a short time. The first time I came I just thanked you for emptying the ashes while we were gone and the next time Rory and I came and only stayed long enough to dig a hole for the lowerpot which had toppled over. I am sorry you did not go with me when I picked out the burial plots. Rose Lawn Memorial park is divided into sections. Each section has a name. Our plot is in the Garden of Gethsemane. I have not purchased a headstone yet, but I plan to do so before Father's Day.

Before I inquire about what you are doing, let me tell you a bit more about what is going on here. You have been getting a lot of mail. You have all kind of credit card offers. Bank of America sent one today, with checks ready to spend. And then, of course, there are those never-ending charities that just keep on asking. Today you received a letter from Boy's Town. You know you always gave a donation to Boy's Town. They sent you a certificate of citizenship. The certificate reads as follows;

BOY'S TOWN
Certificate of
2009 Honorary Citizenship Having
completed all the requirements
And procedures attached thereto
FLORENCE L. MINTER
Is hereby proclaimed a citizen of Boy's
Town Given under my hand and seal
This first day of January, 2009
The certificate is signed by Father Steven
F. Bowes National Executive Director

Now isn't that a nice certificate. After all these years of your giving, you had never gotten a certificate of citizenship or any other kind of certificate. I will write and thank them for you, but I will tell them that they are a little bit late; that your citizenship is *now in heaven. I am sure they will understand why you declined.*

Since you left, we have had some really cold weather. We had an ice storm that closed school for two days. I go to the center almost every day and play dominoes. Junior Boy has also started coming every day. He is doing good with his drug rehab. Wash promised to come by and get a memorial program but he has not done so yet. Your leaving has really been hard for him. You know one of his daughters committed suicide about six months ago.

Donald did not come to the funeral or to the funeral home to see you. He said he wanted to remember you the way you were when you were alive. Your going home services were really nice and the programs were awesome. I chose a picture from the front with you wearing your overalls. There were also other pictures inside the program, showing precious memories of our lives together.

The weather continued to be very cold, but God smiled on us the day of your home going. The day was beautiful. It was so hard to say goodbye.

I know all of your friends and loved ones were glad to see you. This is my version of what happened. Your sister Willie Mae stopped cooking, threw her pot down and came to welcome you. Your sister, Wiloza, was in the choir singing when she saw you and stopped right in the middle of the song to welcome her baby brother home. Wiloza occupied a front row seat in the heavenly choir, just as she did at home in the Pleasant Grove Baptist Church choir. Kat, your oldest brother, was standing at attention in his army uniform and broke rank when he saw you. Gen, the sister you lived with until she died, from childbirth, was still holding her new born baby in her arms, but held out one arm to greet you.

Your mother, Tassie and your niece, Tassie Vada, were walking down Halleluiah Boulevard, on their way to Sunday church, when Tassie looked up and saw you coming down the road. She said hello to you and called you by name. When your mother heard your name, she looked up and saw you. She had not recognized you because you were only two years old when she passed.

What a great reunion it was. She could not get enough hugging and looking at you. It was a happy time for everyone. They went on to church, shouting every step of the way. She told everyone about seeing her baby boy.

Your brother-in-law, Thomas, was painting your room for you and had almost finished when he saw you coming. He rushed to meet you, with his paintbrush in his hands, smearing paint on your beautiful new clothes.

And then there was Joe landers. He looked at you and said, "Man, where have you been?" What took you so long?" Joe asked you about the Friendly Five Gospel Singers that he had managed. You told them they were still singing and that they had come to see you at home and in the nursing home and sang for you. And how much you enjoyed them. And then there was my brother l.V., who lived close to you when you were growing up. He was like an older brother to you. l.

V. and my mother were together when they looked up and saw you. After exchanging hellos, my mother told you how she had told me to never leave you and that she was glad that I had kept my promise. She said one day I would join you; it will be a grand time. She said, "The next time you get together, it will be forever."

The Answer

Dear Dorothy Jean,

I received your letter today and was very glad to hear from you. You were right, I thought you'd never write. The things you told me really did happen, but there was so much more. let me tell you more about what happened.

When I arrived in heaven, I could hear the music playing before I got to the gate. It was the most beautiful music that I had ever heard. Some of the songs were familiar and some were not, but they were all uplifting and reverent. There was a large crowd present at the gate to greet me. The gates into the Holy City are made of pure gold. Some of the biblical characters that we read about in the bible along with some friends I knew were there. They introduced themselves to me and welcomed me into heaven.

I saw Abraham, Isaac and Jacob. I saw the three Hebrew boys who were put in the fiery furnace. I even saw Peter, who was still talking about denying Christ. There are no electric lights up here in heaven. I don't have to worry about paying the light bill. Jesus is the light of the Holy City. There is also no night here. The streets are paved with gold and my new body is perfect. All the sores are gone. All my limbs are working. It is too wonderful to put into words.

I love it here, and I'm sure you will too. There is no more pain here. There is no more sorrow here. Every day is sweeter than the day before. If I had a chance to come back, I would say no. As great as every thing has been, the best is yet to come. As of this writing, I have not met Jesus, but I can feel his presence. I want to see him for myself. I want

49

to see him face to face. I want to personally thank him for dying on the cross, so that I could have a chance to experience this moment. I thank God for His precious gift of Jesus Christ, the greatest gift of all. Goodbye for now. When you get to heaven, I hope I can meet you at the gate. Until then, Just keep on trusting God.

Love,
Florence

Dear Florence,

Saturday February 7, will be our 54th wedding anniversary. How I wish you were here to share it with me, when I come to the Memorial park on Saturday, I will read you this letter.

Today is February 6. Tomorrow is the big day, our 54th wedding anniversary. The last time you were able to take me out to eat was in 2006. We went to Red Lobster. Little did we know it would be the last time going out on our anniversary? Perhaps, if we had known, we would have lingered a little while longer.

The next year, we had planned to go out, but on that day you were not feeling well. Remember, you gave me some money and I went to Applebee's and bought two steak dinners. Just being together was the main thing, not where we were. You know we both liked Applebee's food.

When I come to see you tomorrow, I am bringing some new flowers for your grave. I ordered them for spring, but I will place them on your grave tomorrow before I read the letter. They are beautiful tulips. I ordered them from Starcrest, one of you favorite catalog companies. I also ordered a few other items. I remember how you loved to order things from the catalog. You ordered me a new set of pots and pans that I really needed. Remember the shelf you ordered for our bathroom. You were always finding things to make our home more livable and comfortable. I know they miss your business.

David started plowing yesterday. He is getting ready to plant greens, onions and irish potatoes. Remember how you loved to garden.

We really need some rain. It is very dry. The weathermen say we will get some rain in three or four days. We really need the rain, if our garden is going to do any good.

David still has his chickens. They don't lay many eggs, but he keeps them anyway.

Several people wanted to buy your truck, but I am not going to sell it. David and Rory drive it sometimes, but most of the time, it stays parked under the shed. I bought new license tags and David put them on today before he drove to the store to get gas for the tiller.

Love, Your wife,
Dorothy Jean

I Forgot the Kleenex

It was finally February 7, our anniversary. I had planned my day the night before. I was going to do my errands first and then try to be at the grave site no later than one p.m. When I got up that morning, my plans changed. I made the grave site my first stop on my agenda. Somehow, I began to feel a "pity party" coming on, so I had intended to put some Kleenex in my purse before I left, but I forgot. Just the thought of going to the grave site, especially on our anniversary, made me sad. I had put a copy of the letter in the car the night before and the next morning I took the new flowers and put them in the car.

I left the house about ten thirty a.m. It was a spring like day in the middle of winter. The weatherman had forecasted a high of 77 degrees for the day. It was partly cloudy and 66 degrees when I left home.

The grave site is about a five-minute drive from our house. It was Saturday and there was very little traffic was on the streets. I struggled to keep back the tears all the way. My eyes filled with tears before I arrived. Then I remembered, "I forgot the Kleenex".

When I arrived at the cemetery, I passed the Garden of Gethsemane, where he was buried. I was looking for a grave with a mound, but they had flattened it. It only took a minute for me to realize that I had gone too far. When I arrived at the grave site, I took the flowers and a copy of the letter and walked over to the grave, which was a very short distance. I had planned to change the flowers, but the existing flowers were still very pretty, so I just added the new flowers. After placing the flowers on the grave, I began to read the letter and the pity party was truly on.

I was glad I had chosen to go early. I had the entire Memorial Park all to myself. I cried as long as I needed to; wiping the tears on the sleeve of my jacket and the back of my hand, because I forgot the kleenex. I went back to my car and continued to cry for awhile.

Finally, I looked in my purse and there at the very bottom was a napkin. I took it and cleaned my face before I drove away from the grave site.

I stopped at the office on the way out to pick up some brochures to take home. I wanted the children to help me pick out a monument for his grave. The marker will be a twin marker for him and me.

I finished my errands by one and was back home. It was absolutely, without a doubt, the longest day of my life. I thought about going out to eat or to a movie, but I really did not want to go anywhere.

I don't know how soon I will go again. It made me feel so sad. Is this a good thing to create situations that make you cry?

Tomorrow will be Valentine's Day. I am trying to decide whether or not I am going to see him. I haven't felt very well today. I had some surgery done on my gums and the medicine upset my stomach.

I ordered an electric fireplace and it came today. It is very pretty and throws out a lot of heat.

Today is Valentine's Day. I decided to go to the grave site and take some flowers. I stood there and tried to think of something to say. Finally, I just said,"I love you and happy Valentine's Day."

Our baby son, Rory, came to spend the night. He slept on the couch that was next to the chair where my husband always sat and I do mean *always* sat. The next morning he asked me if the chair squeaked when no one was sitting in it. He informed me that he awoke and the chair was squeaking. I told him I guess his dad had come back to visit. He smiled and said, "I guess so."

I keep remembering the little things that seemed so insignificant when he was alive, but have taken on a whole new meaning now that he is gone.

I can still hear him coming into the house, always whistling and walking with his walking cane. You could always hear it clicking. I remember all the vacations we took and how we enjoyed just being together. I remember how happy he was when he was hired at General Motors. At last, he had a good paying job with benefits. It made him proud to be better able to support his family. I had graduated from college two years earlier and was teaching, but he made more at General Motors than I did teaching.

This was in the year 1964. We had bought two city lots and were building a house on one of the lots. Florence did the taping and bedding of the sheetrock and laid the brick. He would leave his construction job and go directly to work on our house. It was during the time he was laid off and working on the house that a man by the name of Coach Collins came by and told him about the job at General Motors.

Today is April 21, 2009. I have only been to the grave site twice since Valentine's day. The last time I went, I felt so sad. I plan to go back in the near future. How can I stay away? I did not go on Easter Sunday, even though I felt that I should have.

I continue to dream about him every night. Some of the dreams are so beautiful. Oh, if I only had "Just One More Night." But the dreams and memories are all I have.

I am still waiting for the headstone to arrive. Hopefully, it will be here before Father's Day.

Today is Mother's Day. I went to visit the grave site. It was late in the afternoon. The sun was just about to fall behind the western horizon. There was a brisk breeze blowing on my face. I wanted to talk to him, but I did not have very much to say. Finally, I told him about my Mother's Day and how all the kids were home except Rory, and he was coming the next day. He came the next day and took me out to eat. I enjoy spending time with my sons or just looking at them. I can see my husband in all of them. It makes me glad and it also makes me sad. Sometimes, I try to turn back the hands of time, but sooner or later, reality kicks in.

Today is Memorial Day. It has been two weeks since I visited the grave site. The marker finally came and has been set at the grave site. On his side of the marker, is a pointer bird dog and on my side there are praying hands.. The inscription reads: "Together Forever."

My baby boy, Rory, and his family met me at the grave site. The other children showed no interest in coming so I did not suggest that they come. I took new flowers. They were his favorite color (blue). I did have a small pity party before I left for the cemetery. It came on and before I knew it, I was crying. Oh, if I only had, "Just One More Night." The sadness that came over me was overwhelming, but thank God, who is able to keep me from falling, it didn't last long.

My husband liked holidays, especially the summer months. He loved to barbecue for his family and invite friends over. Everyone who knew us, knew if they dropped in, there would be enough for them to eat.

So now I have experienced my first Christmas, wedding anniversary, Valentine's Day, Birthday, Mother's Day and Memorial Day without him. It's like going on the same journey, but traveling a different road.

Today is September 11, 2009. It is hard to believe that it has been eight years since the bombing of the World Trade Center. I went to a retired teacher's meeting and they allowed me to read a poem I had written about 911. Another first has been added.

Monday was Labor Day. As usual, we had more food than we could eat. Last year on Labor Day, he was home, but confined to his bed. His caregiver came and got him up in his special chair and he sat there for about six hours. He enjoyed it so much and was not ready to go back to bed.

We tried to get him up at least once a week, but sometimes, he did not care to get up. We always let it be his decision.

I don't go to the grave site as much as I used to. It always leaves me so sad and empty.

My husband is like God, in that I see him everywhere I go and in everything I do. He is always there with me in my thoughts.

I have not written much during the last three months. I have been just working on a school project. But I continue to dream about him often and some of those dreams have been very intimate and seemed so real.

God answers my prayers and just keeps on giving me, "Just One More Night." Sometimes I just sit and try to relive the good times. Life is a precious gift and we should savor every moment; take every opportunity to show your friends and family how much you love them; for it is later than you think. Never let pride get in the way of your decision. Forgiveness is the key to a happy life. Jesus forgives us for our sins and we must forgive others who mistreat us.

It is September now and the days are growing shorter and the nights are growing longer.

Each day brings me closer to the day that I will join him. The double marker reminds me that I will be together with him in death; our bodies at the grave site and our souls in heaven.

CHAPTER 9

The Relationship

During the early spring of 1977, I began to notice a change in Florence. He usually stayed home during the week when he came home from work. He had first been on the night shift at General Motors, but he was now on the day shift. He started going out on Tuesday and Friday nights just like clock work.

It was at that time that I began to pay attention to the change in his habits. One Friday night, I sat on the porch and waited for him to come home. He came home very late and the next morning when I was sorting the clothes to wash, I found a T-shirt with powder and lipstick on it. It was in early April, about a month or so before college turned out for the summer. He made up a lie about it being a college girl and she was leaving to go home for the summer. I cannot tell you how it made me feel for him to tell me that; just like it was no big deal.

I wanted to accept what he said as truth; that it was just a one time fling, but his behavior did not change. Every Tuesday and Friday nights he had some place to go that did not include me. It was quite evident that he was seeing someone ,and I tried to figure out who in the world it could be.

One Sunday a widow lady came to church. Her husband had been dead for a few years, I think. He was a member of my church, but she belonged to another church. She had visited this church before, but it had been a long time.

Rumor had it that her husband was unfaithfull and she had suffered behind him just as I was suffering. At that time, I had no idea she was the one. But after that day, no matter where I went, I could see her image before me, wearing the gray suit she was wearing on that day. I tried to dismiss her from my mind, but to no avail. She was there before me, no matter where I was. I had prayed and asked God to show me who it was. Was this his sign? Surely this nice lady, who had been through the same thing, would not do this.

In the meantime, I asked my friends and my children if they knew who it was and they pretended they knew nothing.

During that time I was Director of Special Education and had an hour off for lunch. On this particular day, I came home for lunch

While I was there, my middle son, Donald, came by. I had already asked him earlier that year if he knew anything and he said, "No." "So I said,"Donald, I know who your daddy is seeing." And he said, "Who mama?" I told him who it was and he said that I was right. He wanted to know how I had found out, and I told him that God had revealed it to me by placing her image before me every where I went. Then he told me how he had seen them together in the truck.

When I confronted my husband about it, he denied it at first, but finally admitted it. He then tried to give a valid reason. He said he could talk to her without the stress of marriage. He said I did not want to do things with him that he liked to do; namely go to the country to share intimate moments. My main reason for not wanting to go was the competition of the mosquitoes. They took all the pleasure out of whatever you were doing.

He also told me how it got started. He said he was passing her house one day and she was washing her car. He stopped and made a pass at her and asked her for a date and she said yes.

I decided I would talk to her, woman to woman. So one day I passed her house and she was standing in the yard. I told her I knew she was seeing my husband and how God had revealed it to me. I also told her I had a hard time believing that she was the one, because I remembered how her husband had cheated on her.

My trying to stop them only made it worse. The only consolation I had was that he always took care of his family; making sure bills were paid and that there was plenty of food in the house. Of course, I was working and could have managed without him. But through it all, I wanted our marriage to work. I loved him so much and could not imagine my life without him.

It was on May 6 of the same year. Donald had married and was expecting a baby. It was on a Friday afternoon and I had promised to buy him a cook stove. We left home about four in the afternoon to go shopping for a stove. Florence was usually late coming home on Fridays because he would cash his check and go pay all of the bills that were due that week. Donald and I first went to Western Auto and could not find a suitable stove; so we decided to go to Sears.

When we walked in the store, there was my husband, shopping in the women's negligee department. The clerk was holding up a beautiful long blue negligee, getting ready to put it in a box . We hurried to the back of the store to the appliance department so that Florence would not see us. I thought he was buying it for me for Mother's Day and I did not want to spoil his surprise.

Sunday morning came and to my surprise, when I opened the box, there was a short, white negligee. The blue one had been for his girlfriend.

On special days, he would sometimes try to divide his time between us. On the nineteenth of June that year, he left early to be with her and came back later to take me out. I went with him down to the cafe in Shacktown, even though I knew he had been with her.

Isn't that a sad commentary? He had told me that it was all over, but I knew that he was lying. So I tried to think of a way to catch him in the act. This was not that hard to do because he was so predictable.

In July of that same year our grandson, Donald Jr., was born. He was almost two months premature. The baby was still in the hospital when my big day came.

My cousins were in college and I told them what my plans were. I told them that Friday night was the night. I needed Brenda to help carry out my plan. He had told me earlier in the week that he had to go to McKinney on Friday to see about some insurance. Somehow I knew he was lying.

On August 19, I rented a car and parked it at my cousin's apartment. I came home from work that day as usual but remembered that I needed to go to the post office. When I left the post office, I passed a phone booth and there he was, making a phone call. I was sure he was making a date with his girlfriend. I went home and called my cousin.

He was not in McKinney, seeing about insurance, he was making a date. I drove over to my cousin's apartment and picked up the car. I dressed up like a man and my cousin was sitting in the car as if she were my girlfriend. I had figured out that she would probably leave home in her car and meet him in a certain place, but I did not know where. So, I put on my man's hat, a false mustache and a man's dress coat.

Then my cousin and I drove to the street where she lived and waited to see if she would leave. About sundown, she backed out of her driveway and left. We followed her. She drove out Highway 380 to the red barn parking lot and we were not far behind her. Who do you think was waiting for her? My husband of course. She parked her car, hopped out and got in the truck with him. I could have stopped them then, but I wanted to catch them in the act. We followed them as long as we could without them knowing they were being followed. We finally lost them and had to end our pursuit.

We decided to come back to town and get my son and go back to the red barn. We let the air out of all her tires before they got back.

What an emotional time this was. I knew they were together, making love in the country, the way we used to. I guess she did not mind the mosquitoes.

When we arrived at the red barn and pulled up in the parking lot, they were just getting back to the parking lot. They were standing by the truck, saying their goodbyes.

When I walked toward them they finally realized it was me. We exchanged a few harsh words. My husband grabbed my arms to keep me from hitting her. My son grabbed my husband and pulled him away from me. Remember, the air had been let out of her tires and they were all on flat, so she had to drive slowly, all the way home.

We followed her all the way home, with my husband behind us. He had his pistol with him and told us when we arrived at her house that if we messed with her, he would kill us all.

This should have been enough for me to give up on the relationship, but it wasn't. As I look back on it now, I don't know how I managed to stay and keep my sanity.

The relationship continued for the next three years. We would run into each other from time to time and exchange a friendly greeting.

On another occasion, he came home after being with her and told me she said that I had come by her house and cursed her granddaughter, who she said was in the yard.

When he confronted me about it, I had no idea what he was talking about. It was a total lie. We were in the kitchen when he confronted me about it. I went into the bed room and he followed me, shoved me down on the bed, calling me a liar; that he knew his girlfriend was telling the truth. As I look back on it now, I believe he was lying on her and needed an excuse to pick a fight.

It just so happened that God gave me the strength to get up from the bed. There was a lamp on the dresser behind him, and I managed to pick it up and hit him over the head with it. That was the end of that fight. He told me he would never bother me again.

Can you believe that we both slept in the same bed that night? No, we did not make love, but we slept side by side.

The only difference was that I went into the kitchen and got a sharp knife and put it between the mattresses on my side of the bed. He was back on the night shift at this time, so the next morning, when I went to work, I forgot to take the knife back to the kitchen. When he got up later that morning and made up the bed, he found the knife. When I came home for lunch, I was going to take the knife back to the kitchen. When I looked up he was watching and wanted to know what I was looking for; that he had found the knife when he made up the bed. I told him that I had put it there and that if he had attempted to bother me in any way, I was going to separate his head from his body.

This seemed to get his attention. He began to act a little bit afraid of me for a long time. He even thought I might try to poison him.

He did, however, continue his relationship. He even had the nerve to tell me one time that he had seen this guy on the street and he wanted to know how he could be so lucky to get her to date him. He supposedly at one time had dated her. Can you imagine the nerve of him saying that to me?

One summer, we were going to San Antonio on vacation. It was the day before we were to leave. I came home for lunch that day and he had already left. Something told me that he had gone to work early so that he could meet her at a motel before he went to work. He could not leave town without seeing her. He knew he would be gone several days.

I left home and went to Dallas to try and find them. At some point had found a hotel card among his things so I had a pretty good idea where they would be. When I got to the hotel, they had already been there and left.

I rushed back to Denton and sure enough, when I came down Loop 288, there she was in her car getting ready to make a left turn. I pulled up behind her so fast that I was unable to stop, so I hit her from behind. She got out of the car and saw who it was. I told her I knew she had been with my husband and she said they had only been to the movies.

After I hit her car, she decided not to go home, but went in a different direction. I did not tell my husband about the incident, but of course, she did. He told me he was going to have her car fixed.

We went to San Antonio on vacation, but it was not a happy time.

After that, I thought I had finally had enough. I filed for divorce, but could not go through with it.

Finally, in the spring of 1980, he came to me and told me that we had come to the end of the road and he was leaving and moving to Dallas where he would be close to his job. He found an apartment close to our daughter and she helped him pick out his furniture for the apartment.

CHAPTER 10

The Apartment

On April 1, 1980, Florence moved into his apartment in Dallas. I gave him some of my kitchenware and packed it for him. That was a very sad day for me. When he left that Saturday afternoon, I thought my heart was breaking, but I never asked him not to leave. In the mean time, my daughter had invited the family to dinner at her house. This was the next day after he moved into his apartment.

My husband called our daughter and told her that he wanted to come. She called me because she did not want me to think she was taking sides. I had already told her it was OK whatever she did for her daddy when she helped him pick out the furniture.

Florence only lived about 10 minutes away from our daughter, so the next day when we arrived from Denton, Florence was already there. He was so proud of his apartment and insisted that we all go by to see his apartment on his way home.

When we left our daughter's house, we all went by his apartment. I went into his bedroom and cried. No one saw or heard me but this whole experience was just too much for me.

It was as if I were living a nightmare and soon I would awaken and we would all be back home together, with all of the pain behind us.

He was acting like I was his sister instead of the wife he had left. He had always lived with someone else until he got married and maybe having his own place had a special meaning for him. At any rate , he was there and I was at our home in Denton.

After he moved out, he filed for divorce, but never pursued it any further. As far as I know, his girlfriend from Denton never went down there to his apartment. He came back home every weekend just like he was working out of town during the week and coming home for the weekend. He would come for the weekend and go back on Monday morning.

He had a brief relationship with a younger woman, but it did not last long.

On the weekends that he did not come home, I went to his apartment. Isn't that strange? Here I am, continuing to love him and allowing our relationship to continue, after all that had happened.

I did not understand it then and I do not understand it now. Yes, love is a strange bedfellow. It promotes stupidity, it overrides your pride. I prayed and asked God to take away my love for him, but to no avail.

After he moved away and started coming back, he stayed close to home. I'm not saying that he never saw his girlfriend who lived in Denton, but since he spent most of his time at home, I don't think he saw very much of her.

Also, during all of the years that he had this relationship with her, there were rumors that she had other suitors. All I know for sure is that every Tuesday and Friday nights were their nights.

I told him when he left that I would never ask him to come back home to stay, and if he ever wanted to come back, he would have to ask me.

After about six months, he started talking about tearing out the wall between the two smaller bedrooms and making one big bedroom. He also said that he wanted to come back. I told him that he could do the remodeling and move back home.

I also need to say that when he first started coming home for the weekend, we did not immediately resume our married relationship. He slept on the couch in the den. I guess this was my way of playing a little bit hard to get.

In June of that year, I went to Europe for two weeks and asked him to stay in the house while I was gone. When I came back, he just kept on staying. He would go to work and instead of going to his apartment after work, he would come back to Denton. He finally started staying in his apartment during the week, except for the time it took him to remodel the house. It made a nice master bedroom and he did all of the work himself. The house had only one bath, but he cut a door from the new master bedroom that led directly into the bathroom.

He was supposed to move back at Christmas time, after the master bedroom was finished, but he didn't. By this time I had given him a key to the house. At Christmas time when he was suppose to move in, I came home one day and he had been there and left the house key on the dresser. I saw his truck parked at his sister's house, which was just four doors down the street.

January, February, March and April passed and he had not moved back home. He had also started coming back to the house, but I was not cozy with him. I told him if he had not moved back before the last day of April, he could not move back at all.

He told me that it was in the middle of the week and he did not have time to move. I told him that was fine with me. It was the last day of April; the last day that I was going to allow him to move back. After all, enough is enough and too much stinks, and this situation had been stinking too long.

He left early that morning and went to work and so did I. At least, I thought he went to work. When I went home for lunch that day, much to my surprise, he came around the corner with his truck loaded. He was moving back home.

I was almost mad at myself for letting him move back home, but I was also happy. The children were upset with me for allowing him to move back after he had left me after being unfaithful all these years.

After he moved back home, he resumed his relationship with this same woman, or maybe it never really ended. I just stopped playing detective.

CHAPTER 11

Six Months Gone

Today is June 3, 2009. It was six months ago today thatt my husband passed away. I can still hear the knock on my door. I can still see the nurse standing there with a sad look on her face and telling me that my husband had passed away. And then she quickly added, "He went peacefully."

I can see him lying there in the hospital bed. Even though he was dead, his body was still warm. Only three hours ago, I had hugged and kissed him good night as I always did, and told him that I would see him in the morning. If I had known it was his last night to be alive, I would not have gone to bed.

I guess God did not want me to see him to take his last breath.

I had imagined this moment many times. As I imagined it, I would be holding him in my arms and telling him how much I loved him, and he would respond, if only with his eyes, *I love you too*.

I say with his eyes because it had been three days since he had demonstrated intelligible speech. Three days earlier, he had tried to tell me something. The nurse was there and neither she or I could understand what he was trying to say.

This was the last time he tried to say anything. So why did I not know that his body was shutting down? It was because it had happened several times before and he had rallied. Sometimes, the next day, he would be cracking jokes. When you asked him how he felt, he would say, with a lopsided grin, that he felt with his hands. Sometimes I would say that I felt with my hands too.

So here I am, six months later, remembering the day when our 53 year, 10 month marriage ended.

I Just Had to Write Again

Dear Florence,

Today is June 21, 2009. It is Father's day, the very first one without you. We had our usual Juneteenth Celebration this weekend here in Denton. There were more people here than I had ever seen before. I thought about last year.

Remember, you wanted a chopped beef sandwich. I bought one sandwich and it was enough for both of us. And even though you were mostly being tube fed, except for soft foods, you were able to eat the chopped beef. Do you remember how good it was? I was so afraid you may choke, but you did fine. I was so proud. It almost seemed like old times.

I had not planned to write you again, but I just had to tell you about my trip. I went on a bus trip with the Senior Center. There were two charter buses. They were owned by Diamond Tours. There were 46 people on each bus. Sarah Parker and her husband went on the trip, also Bubba and Lillie Clark, Nell Ridge, who is Lillie Clark's sister, Helen Medcafe and Betty Kimble also went. Betty was my roommate.

I was so anxious to get away. I thought it would help me to not think about you all the time. But I think it made me think of you even more. You, my favorite roommate were not there. I kept wishing you were there with me. I kept remembering the trips we took, whether long or short. Every time we stopped, you would be shopping for hats and bumper stickers.

When I saw the other couples enjoying each other on the trip, I was just a little bit jealous. Oh, what I wouldn't give for "Just One More Night." Our destination was Mackinac, Michigan. It took us two days to get there. We left at eight on June 6.

We spent the first night in Roberts, Missouri. Some of us went to a show that night in a nearby town. It was like the Grand Ole Opry. You would have really enjoyed it.

The next day we left for St. Louis, Missouri, where we visited the famous arch. I had not planned to go inside the arch, but I needed to use the bathroom and there was no outside rest room available. The line was extremely long. I told the guard that I was not going on the tour, but I really needed to use the bathroom. She told me I still had to go to the end of the line. I looked at her and said to myself, "I don't think so."

I rushed to the entrance and was told that I had to go through security and get by bag checked before I could go in. Time was running out for me and I guess this nice man at the head of the line must have seen my desperation. He told security to let me go ahead of him at the front of the line and she did. Guess what! I made it to the bathroom just in the nick of time. We spent the second night in Illinois. I don't remember the name of the town. The next morning, we headed for Michigan, where we spent the next four days.

The next morning, we caught the ferry and went out to Mackinac Island. There were no cars allowed on the island except emergency vehicles. We rode and toured the island in a carriage pulled by horses. There were also bicycles that tourists could rent to tour the island.

The next day we headed for Sault St. Marie, Michigan and took an exciting cruise through the Soo Locks. We also visited several other places of interest. In route home, we visited the Abraham Lincoln Presidential Museum. The things we saw there opened many of the old wounds of slavery. There were people crying and others who chose not to look at certain displays. I did some shopping at the museum store.

How I wish you could have been there. Yes, there were souvenir hats to buy and I know you would have bought one.

Today, as I said earlier in the letter, is Fathers Day. I went to the grave site and took you some flowers. You know, I told you about the headstone. It says: Florence L. and Dorothy J. Minter, Together Forever. *Somehow, just seeing my name there by yours is very comforting. It makes me feel closer to you somehow. I never stay long when I go to the grave site and I only go about twice a month.*

It has taken me so long to write this letter. It is now the fifth of July. Yesterday was the fourth of July. David really made some good barbecue. Rory and his family are living with us now. It is good to have him home. They rented their house in Kingsville and are looking at houses in Denton and also somewhere near his job in Haltom City.

Today is Sunday. After church today, I went to visit your grave. It had rained earlier in the day and the flowers looked so fresh and beautiful. As I entered the memorial park, the flowers, in all of their beauty, seemed to be saying, "All is well, all is well."

Guess what! Another pity party. I thought I had everything under control. I walked up to the grave, talked to you for a bit and went back to the car. Just as I was about to sit down in the car, it hit me. I cried until I felt relieved. Then I drove back home. Oh, if I only had "Just One More Night."

Love, Your wife
Dorothy Jean

CHAPTER 12

The Bipolar Years

During the same time period from 1977 to 1990, Florence was diagnosed with bipolar disease. The stress of his relationship with this woman seemed to trigger it.

There were many bipolar episodes during these years. He was treated and confined at treatment centers several times during those years.

There was a treatment center in Denton and sometimes he would admit himself. He found out if you admit yourself, you could sign yourself out.

As a young man, he was very shy and somewhat withdrawn. This may have been a manifestation of the low end of bipolar. He also had a secondary diagnosis of schizophrenia. At one point, at the height of his infidelity, he was afraid to eat my food. He thought I was trying to poison him.

He never forgave me for having him admitted to treatment centers under court order. He always brought that up and would say he was going to kill me if he ever got out. On one occasion, I stayed in a shelter for abused women because he was looking for me to kill me.

One of the reasons his girlfriend broke up with him was out of fear.

He even had the nerve to tell me that she wouldn't talk to him because she was afraid of me. I told him she was not afraid of me; she was afraid of him.

In the following pages, I will recall in detail some of the frightening experiences I had during some of his bipolar episodes. It would be like a demon had entered his body and taken over his soul. There was no reasoning with him. He was violent and overbearing. He drove recklessly and drank excessively during these periods. It is a true miracle that he did not hurt himself or someone else with his drunk driving.

He also had an obsession with guns. He owned two pistols and four shotguns. We never went anywhere unless he carried his gun.

Before I go any further, I need to tell you a little bit about bipolar illness, so that you can really understand what is going on.

Bipolar disorder is a mood disorder that affects one in every 70 people and puts them at risk for all kinds of problems in their family, social and work lives. People with bipolar disease are also at high risk for physical problems, alcohol, substance abuse and even suicide.

First, let me define the syndrome of bipolar disorder. It is defined by severe mood swings, from manic highs to severe depression. It is a mood disorder, because it profoundly affects a person's experiences of emotion and "affect," which is the way one conveys emotion to others. It is called bipolar because the mood swings occur between two poles, high and low.

In the manic, "high" state, people experience different combinations of the following: elated or euphoric mood (excessive happiness or expansiveness), irritable mood, (excessive anger and touchiness), a decreased need for sleep, grandiosity or an inflated sense of themselves and their abilities, increased talkativeness and racing thoughts. Their thoughts jump from one thing to another. There is a huge increase in energy levels. They also display reckless and impulsive behavior.

The episodes that I am about to describe, took place over a 10-year period. The episodes are not necessarily in chronological order. Most of the episodes occurred during the spring and summer.

The Episodes

It was during the month of March. Florence came home very angry. You could always tell when he was going into the manic state. His activity level would increase by 100 percent. He would become very abusive and accusatory.

On this particular night he came home and accused me of something. For the life of me, I cannot remember what it was. Suffice it to say that when I refused to admit to whatever it was, he drew two pistols on me; one on each side of my head. He made me get down on my knees and told me if I moved he would blow my brains out. He took my glasses off so that I would not be able to see as well as I needed to.

When he left, I called a friend across town and she let me come and stay with her for a few days. All the while he was looking for me, he thought I was at my son's house.

A few days later, I came back to the house to get some more clothes. He had destroyed our bedroom. To make things worse, he came home while I was there and tried to harm me. About that time, my second son came home and told him he had better not harm me. As a matter of fact, he held him off me while I got my clothes.

During the same time period, Florence had decided to go into the used car business. He would drive some of the cars until he could sell them.

A few weeks prior to this, I had Florence committed to Wichita Falls State Hospital in Wichita Falls, Texas. They sent him back home after three days for a hearing. We went to court and he convinced the court that he was OK. I begged them to keep him confined for treatment, but they refused.

I decided to move in with my son and his family. He and his family lived in an apartment about two miles from our house. I parked my car a few blocks away from the apartment, so that Florence would not know that I was there. David always left for work early in the morning about six.

The neighbors saw my husband sitting outside the apartment in one of the old cars that he had bought to resell. He was flashing a gun so they called the police. When the police came, he shot at them. He woke up when the police fired back at him. He crunched down in the floorboard of the car. The police shot into the car 35 times. Then the ambulance came and took him to the hospital emergency room.

I just knew he was dead. It is truly a miracle that he wasn't killed. His injuries consisted of a bullet hole through his left hip and his left arm. His arm required surgery.

When I got to the hospital, the police were ready to take him to jail. I reminded them that only a few days ago, I had begged them to send him back to Wichita Falls State Hospital for treatment and they had refused. Now, they wanted to take him to jail when he needed treatment. I told them they were not going to take him to jail. They, at my request, called his psychiatrist and he ordered that he be admitted to the hospital for treatment. So they took him to Flow Hospital in Denton.

One of the reasons treatment was never successful is because he would not stay on his medication.

Between the years of 1977 and 1985, he was hospitalized several times. He was confined to Wichita Falls State Hospital three times. He went to Presbyterian Hospital twice. His other hospitalizations was at the Flow Hospital behavioral unit.

He was always angry with me, and I don't think he ever did forgive me for having him hospitalized. He never believed he had a problem or at least he never admitted he had a problem.

During his manic episodes, he would go on a gambling spree. As a matter of fact, for a few years, he gambled almost every weekend. One weekend he drove my car to the gambling house. I knew he drove my car but I did not know he came home without it until a friend of ours called and told me he had lost my car in a card game. He told me where the car was and who had won it. I had another set of keys.

The man who won it lived about five minutes away from our house. I had someone drop me off. I told the man that Florence could not sell the car because it belonged to me and he would have to settle the debt with my husband. He said OK and I got in my car and drove home.

I can't even remember what I said to Florence about the incident, because if he were that far gone, there would be no reasoning with him. As I look back on those years, I can't believe I actually continued to stay in the relationship.

As I have said before, many times I prayed to God for him to take away my love for him, but no matter how many times I prayed that prayer, I could not stop loving him. 'Till death do us part was a true reality in my life. Each of us filed for divorce once, but we never followed through.

Today is October 2, 2009. Tomorrow will be the 10-month anniversary of his death. I haven't been to the grave site in almost a month. Now that fall is here, I need to change the flowers on his grave. I want to pick something real pretty for fall.

These 10 months have passed so quickly. This time last year he was here at home in his hospital bed. God has blessed me by allowing me to dream beautiful dreams of us being together. The dreams are so wonderful, and even though I know they are only dreams, I look forward to each and every one. And no matter how many dreams I have, I continue to wish for "Just One More Night."

I continue to sleep in the same bed that we shared for many years. Sometimes, I look over to his side of the bed and try to imagine him there with me. As a matter of fact, I see him everywhere.

We have had some unexplainable occurrences since he passed away. My sons always say, "Daddy did that."

It took me a while to get used to so many caregivers coming and going. I also think he was uncomfortable with so much exposure to his privacy. He required total care. Sometimes when they would come, he would play possum. One caregiver was surprised to know that he could talk.

I continue to have my pity parties ever so often. Crying has a healing affect on my soul. When my heart feels heavy and sad, a good cry leaves me feeling much better.

Sometimes I stand and gaze at his pictures on the wall. Then I remember the events and circumstances associated with each photograph. We have a lot of family pictures.

People suffering from bipolar disease are fearless.

They think the law does not apply to them.

You know there is a law that prohibits the discharge of firearms within the city limits. When my husband was in one of his bipolar episodes, he decided to go hunting in the city limits. Not only was it in the city limits but also it was near a school that is next door to our property.

The police caught him and arrested him. He posted a $2,500 cash bond and did not have to stay in jail. He hired a lawyer who was going to charge him $2,500 to handle his case. He had to report to the court from time to time.

One day he left the house and told me he had to go meet with his lawyer. About an hour later, the phone rang. It was a friend of ours calling to tell me that Florence had been taken to jail; the police had caught him hunting in a park near an apartment complex. Not only was he hunting, but he had also killed a squirrel and it was in the back of the truck. The friend said I needed to come and get the truck before they picked it up to take it to the pound. I was so disgusted. I did not do anything right away. By the time I decided to go and get the truck, it had been taken to the pound.

At some point, he got mad at his lawyer and fired him. He said all the lawyer wanted was to get his hands on his money. The courts were still holding his $2,500. I decided to go and talk to the District Attorney. She told me if he waived his right to a lawyer, he would only have to pay his court costs. So he met all of his court dates, stayed out of trouble during his probationary period and was given back his $2,500.

The police department knew him personally. They knew about his condition. He could get away with anything short of murder.

He also had problems on his job. When he was sick, he would refuse to work and use very abusive language when talking to his superiors. I found out from some of the other men who lived in Denton and worked for General Motors that he was about to loose his job. So I called the office and talked to his boss and explained his condition. He was able to take disability leave for several months. During his leave, he was confined to the hospital for treatment.

When he was well enough, he went back to work. As I look back on those years, I realize that it was a true miracle that he was able to work at General Motors for about 28 years. He retired in 1993.

CHAPTER 13

Eleven Months Gone

It has been eleven months since my husband passed away. It is hard to believe that it has been that long. With each season, come new memories.

He looked forward to this time of the year when he could go bird hunting. It is early December.

Even though he was crippled and had to use a cane, he would somehow kill a mess of birds. He had trained his dogs to retrieve his birds and bring them to him. He also liked to cook them. He would fry them nice and crisp. He would also make brown gravy to go with them.

He would cook some canned biscuits and eat them with some ribbon cane syrup. He liked to cook and he always enjoyed feeding other people. I guess that was a carryover from his country upbringing. In the country, we fed everybody who came along and was hungry. As a matter of fact, our parents would be insulted if you didn't eat. We both grew up in the country, so we were on the same wavelength as it related to feeding people.

I also remember how he would plant a fall garden and hope the harvest would come before the frost. He grew some of the biggest sweet potatoes you have ever seen. We also had greens and green beans that we harvested in the fall as well as the spring and summer.

I can still see him on the tractor, mowing the yard. Sometimes he would drive so fast when he was mowing the grass, I was afraid he was going to turn over.

When the temperature dropped below 50 degrees, he was ready to build a fire in the fireplace. I think I already mentioned the big fires he would build in the fireplace. He would place so much wood on the fire that the flames would go way up into the chimney. Also, sometimes he would place a stick of wood in the fireplace that was too long. So he would just let it hang out and as it burned, he would move it further up into the fireplace. This caused the room to become smoky, but he was determined to do it his way.

We had a smoke alarm that was a part of our security system and the smoke would set off the fire alarm, bringing the fire trucks to our house, only to find a smoking fireplace. They finally stopped coming, but would call to make sure everything was all right.

So today, these precious memories flood my soul. I remember us sitting by the fire on those cold winter nights and watching television. I remember how we both would go to sleep before the end of the movie and each would want to know from the other, how it ended. Then we would have a big laugh, realizing that we were both asleep at the end of the movie. How I wish for "Just One More Night."

He even went to sleep at the movies when we were courting. It is so hard sometimes to keep going without him.

When I need to talk, I go to the grave and tell him my problems; Somehow, I know he is listening. I have to believe that. It keeps me feeling closer to him, even though, deep down in my heart, I know that his earthly journey is over.

The other day, I looked in the closet. I still have the log where the caregivers kept a record of everything they did. I reached for it. I was going to look at some of the entries, but I decided that it would be too painful.

Even though he had many good caregivers, it just seemed to take away his dignity, having so many people come and go, taking care of his personal needs. Sometimes he would pretend to be asleep while they were taking care of him. It surprised some of the caregivers when they found out that he could talk, and even had a sense of humor. I sometimes wonder why he did that. Maybe, he felt like if he did not respond, he could pretend they were not there and protect his dignity.

Some talked to him like he was hard of hearing. Some talked to him like he was retarded. But most of them treated him with dignity and respect.

He was so glad to be home. He spent a total of about 300 days in hospitals and nursing homes. He stayed at two different nursing homes. He would stay 100 days and then stay at home for at least 60 days and go to the hospital for three or more days. Then he would qualify for another hundred days in a nursing facility.

Finally, on April 14, 2009, I brought him home to stay. I hired a caregiver and also had hospice for five days a week. In addition to that, my son David and my granddaughter, Carlyon who lived with me at that time, helped me take care of him. The nursing home only gave him a few days to live and so did our family doctor. But God was not ready for him yet. He had such a strong will to live. He told the Chaplain his goal was to get well.

He was tube fed, but once in a while I would give him some soft food. On the nineteenth of June that year, I told him I was going to the park to get me a chopped beef sandwich. As I mentioned earlier, he told me to bring him one. I did not bring him one, but I shared mine, which was more that enough for both of us. He enjoyed that sandwich so much. You could hear him smacking all the way into the other room. I wish I had taken a picture of him, eating that chopped beef sandwich. He had such a happy look on his face. That was the last time he was able to eat barbecue. On Labor Day, my son barbecued. He tried to eat some, but he couldn't.

He went into Respid twice during those eight months.

It was located at Baylor Hospital in Fort Worth, Texas.

CHAPTER 14

Bipolar disorder; A Closer Look

In an earlier chapter, bipolar was briefly discussed. In this chapter, we will take a closer look at bipolar disorder. Perhaps someone in your family may be suffering from an undiagnosed bipolar disorder.

Perhaps you may read something in this disclosure that will help you to get help for someone.

For many years, my husband was not diagnosed. All we knew was, that as a boy, he was always shy and compliant and mannerly. It was not until after we were married that I realized that he had a dark side. He never admitted that he had a problem. He would never try a treatment plan for any substantial length of time.

Treatment for this disorder requires a lifetime commitment to drug therapy.

What is bipolar disorder?

Bipolar disorder, often referred to as manic depression, is a mood disorder, characterized by episodes of clinically significant impairment due to mania or depression.

Bipolar disorder is a serious medical illness. It affects millions of people. Bipolar disorder typically develops in early adulthood, but some people develop symptoms in childhood or late in life. It is often not recognized as an illness or misdiagnosed as depression or attention deficit hyperactive disorder (ADHD). People may suffer for years before they are properly diagnosed and treated. Bipolar disorder is a long-term illness and must be carefully managed throughout a person's life.

There are three types of bipolar disorder outlined by the DSM-IV-TR, and generally accepted within the bipolar community.

Bipolar I and II, like many other disorders involving brain chemistry, are bipolar disorder, which are still under investigation and symptoms may vary significantly from person to person. Typically, symptoms include periods of euphoria, which alternate with periods of profound depression. In most cases, periods of mood stability complement these periods of instability.

The DSM-IV-TR details two general profiles of bipolar disorder: Bipolar I and II. Bipolar I is characterized by alternating episodes of full blown mania and depression, while Bipolar II, the least severe and most common type of the disorder, is characterized by episodes of depression.

Mania and depression are opposing phases in a bipolar disorder.

Mania: A person in a manic phase may feel indestructible, full of energy and ready for anything. At other times, that person may be irritable and ready to argue with anyone who tries to get in their way. Unrealistic plans, spending sprees, an increase in sexual affairs or other reckless behaviors, such as wild driving, may occur. Less sleep and food than usual are needed.

The person with mania can also stay up all night, but may not accomplish much because they are so easily distracted.

The person with bipolar disorder may talk very quickly and jump from subject to subject; they often exhibit pressured speech during mania. Self-esteem may be inflated.

Any decisions made in regard to business and finances, are often not good ones.

Clothing choices may also change, and the person with bipolar disorder may start wearing flashy and more flamboyant clothes.

These behaviors, which can be quite upsetting, usually prompt a family member to take notice and try to get the person help.

Most people going through the manic phase of the disorder deny that anything is wrong with them and refuse to see a medical professional.

They are grandiose and may have delusions of greatness.

Depression: Although mania is said to alternate with depression, more people have depressive episodes than manic ones. The depressive ones may go unnoticed because they do not call attention to themselves in the same way as those in the manic phase.

Sadness and crying spells are common in the depressed phase, but they may isolate themselves; therefore no one knows about it.

People who are depressed may not care enough to wash or comb their hair or even get out of bed in the morning. These people may have trouble sleeping or sleep too much. Many of these people have no interest in food or have no appetite and loose weight; however, some eat excessively.

People with depression have trouble thinking. They may forget to do important things, such as paying a bill because they feel so down. They withdraw from friends.

Hobbies that used to bring pleasure suddenly hold no interest for people who are depressed.

Depression brings feelings of helplessness and hopelessness. People who are depressed may not see the point in living anymore and may actually think about killing themselves.

Some people with the bipolar cycle are between the two extremes every few months or weeks; other people with bipolar may cycle several times within the same day. Social withdrawal and lack of interest in activities were shown in the depressed state.

My husband exhibited all of the behaviors of the manic phase, except the fancy dressing.

(The proceeding discussion related to Bipolar disorder is taken from a variety of unnamed sources on the World Wide Web and are believed to be accurate, realizing that they are not a product of scientific research.)

CHAPTER 15

The Thanksgiving Letter

Dear Florence,

Here I am writing to you again. It is November 22, 2009. Soon it will be a year since you passed away. I went to your grave site today. It had been about six weeks since I had been. The memorial park looked and smelled of fall. The park that only a few weeks ago, showed flowers and green grass now showed an array of leaves that covered the park and spread across the graves. It was a beautiful sight to see. I stood there and took in all the beauty, while I talked to you, trying to catch you up on all the latest. I had a small pity party. My eyes filled with tears, but I left before it became full blown.

I wanted to tell you that I continue to do consultant work for the school. I am spending some of the extra money getting Donald's teeth pulled and new dentures. He has only three good teeth left and is suppose to get them all pulled tomorrow. Medicaid is paying for the extractions, but he has to pay for the examination and dentures. The appointment is tomorrow at 12:45 p.m. and he is afraid. You know this is not like our macho son to be afraid.

You know he is disabled now and cannot work on a regular job. He tries to pick up junk and sell it , but the economy is so bad, and so many people are relying on junk to survive, that junk is scarce.

I also wanted to let you know that people in the community are signing a petition to be presented to the school board to name a school or facility after me. Just think, it will bear the Minter name.

This Thursday will be Thanksgiving. Little did I know that last year would be our last Thanksgiving together. I remember you did not feel like sitting up in your special chair that day, so we let you stay in bed. You had been on continuous care a few days earlier, but you were doing better.

Rory Dean and his family are living with us now. They may be here until spring. They need to sell their house in Kingsville. They are renting it now. David cannot build a fire in the fireplace because it aggravates Timmy's asthma.

Rev. James Cooper and Billy Mitchell died last week. Have you seen them walking around heaven yet? We are planning our Thanksgiving dinner, who is going to cook what. David is making sweet potato pies and banana pudding. Nedra is making her famous cake and macaroni and cheese. Carol is making potato salad and green bean casserole.

I am making turkey, dressing, fruit salad, rolls and gravy. Of course, there will be drinks of all kinds.

Kroger had the best sale; five 12 packs for $11 I finally got your will probated. It was delayed because our lawyer had emergency heart surgery. He is fine now and onery as ever. I am having it all put into a trust, so that when I die the children will not have to go through probate.

An insurance man is trying to get me to, among other things, defer paying my taxes and put the money in some kind of savings that is suppose to yield good returns. He said when I die, the kids could take some of the savings and pay the back taxes. I thought to myself, he has to be crazy or he thinks I am. You know we have always paid our taxes in full the last week in December and I plan to continue doing so. And I know, if I were foolish enough to do that, you would come back and haunt me. You know we always took great pride in paying our bills on time.

I saw Johnny Schrader the other day. I reminded him of that day in 1962, when we brought our baby son Rory home from the hospital and needed milk and other supplies for the baby. We did not have any money. He said he knew we did not have any money, but to get whatever we needed for the baby. He said he knew we would pay him as soon as we could. Remember how proud we were when we could pay him?

Goodbye for now,
Love you and miss you,
Dorothy Jean

P.S. Today is December 13, 2009. Jenell Landers was buried yesterday. You know she had been sick for a long time. She had not done well since Joe passed. So now they are together again, just as we will be someday. Have you seen her yet? I am sure you will flnd her wherever Joe is.

We also lost Dooley Lee last week and a young lady form our church. She had suffered from cancer for a long time.

David has decorated the yard with Christmas decorations. They are so beautiful. You remember how they can be seen for a long way off. Of course,

I'm sure they don't begin to compare with the lights in the Holy City.

Goodbye for now,
Your wife,
Dorothy Jean

CHAPTER 16

The Questionnaire Results

In the process of writing this book, I began to wonder how many women had dealt with some of the same problems I had and how they coped with the situations.

I sent out the questionnaires and received some interesting responses.

I would like to share with you the results of the questionnaire. Because of the number of respondents, the results are not statistically significant. However, they do give some valuable information. A copy of the questionnaire is included in this section

They were not required to give their names. I only wanted the information.

As you can see, the first thing I wanted to know was their age and how long they had been married. Only 10 percent of the respondents were below 50. The youngest was 24.

60 percent of the respondents were between 51 and 75.

30 percent were between 76 and 82.

50 percent of the husbands were deceased and 50 percent were still alive. Only 10 percent of the respondents said their husbands were abusive. Ninety percent said they were not.

Twenty percent of the respondents said their husbands were unfaithful. Eighty percent said their husbands were not unfaithful. Ninety percent of the respondents said they would marry their husbands over again, knowing what they know now.

Ten percent said they would not marry them over again. It was interesting to note that the fact that they were unfaithful or abusive, had nothing to do with whether or not they stayed in the marriage, or would marry them all over again. Fifty percent of the respondents said their husbands were their first choice. Forty five percent said their husbands were not their first choice. Thirty percent of the respondents said they were not their husband's first choice and twenty percent said they did not know. Ninety percent of the respondents said their husbands worked hard to take care of their families.

Only two percent said they were not good providers.

.Ninety five percent of the men were Christians. Only five percent were not Christians.

It is evident from the survey that the determining factor that kept them together may have been the fact that they were good providers, who worked hard to take care of their families.

Being abusive and/or unfaithful did not seem to be a determining factor. It is also interesting to note that being their first choice had nothing to do with whether they would do it all over again.

Questionnaire

Age _____ Yrs. Married _____

Circle one

1. Is your husband still alive?   Yes   No
2. Is or was he abusive?   Yes   No
3. Was he unfaithful?   Yes   No
4. Would you marry him again, knowing what you know now?   Yes   No
5. Was he your first choice?   Yes   No
6. Were you his first choice or do you know?   Yes   No
7. Did he work hard to take care of his family?   Yes   No
8. Was he a Christian?   Yes   No

In your own words, tell me about your marriage and why you stayed or didn't stay. Use the space below to share your thoughts. Use the back of the page, if needed.

(If you would like to be a part of this survey, copy and submit this form to: Dorothy Jean Minter, PO Box 1232, Denton, Texas 76202)

Comments From the Respondents

The following comments were taken directly from the respondents' questionnaires.

Respondent # 1

The respondent indicated that her husband was neither abusive nor unfaithful, but she would not marry him again. This is what she said. "He complained constantly. There seemed to be no way to please him, unless I constantly fed his ego. I think all of this may have been caused by hypertension— not sure. I really do believe he suffered from anxiety neurosis. I stayed because if he or she says he loves me (Christ) and does not keep my teachings, he or she is a liar.

Respondent # 2

This is a no-fault response. He is the kind of husband that would make an excellent clone. This is what she said: "My husband has always been a nice loving husband. He is very generous, almost to a fault. He is a great father to our children and always sets a good example for them and the thousands of students he worked with during his 35 year teaching career."

Respondent # 3

This respondent had some very interesting things to say. When asked if he were unfaithful, she said, "in a way". When asked if she would marry him again, she said, "yes." This is her response, exactly as she wrote it. "I loved my husband very much. He did have problems due to a controlling mother. Probably what drew him to me was my meek personality. It was like he had two personalities. His "good side" was a very loving, kind, slow to anger and very much a Christian man. His "bad side" had sexual hang-ups. I can't prove it, but I think he had sexual encounters with other men. After a few years, there

Just One More Night

were signs of such happenings but I could not face the problem or acknowledge it.

"He never discussed his 'adventures' with me and I guess I didn't want to know. I kept my unanswered questions buried deep inside me. I ignored this behavior for such a long time."

"Much later in our marriage, things were happening in our marriage that brought his 'bad side' out into the open. He did lie to me, trying to cover up his behavior. My children never knew of this behavior until much later.

"I just floated along with my hurt feelings. I guess I was afraid to leave him. He needed professional help and did get some, but it did not stop the problem. I really don't know how often these happenings took place. He kept the secret to himself.

"Now that he is dead, I realize how mad I am with him at his 'bad side.' I feel I am betraying him with this anger. I am angry he didn't correct the problem and talk to me about it. I'm as unhealthy as he was for not facing the problem sooner and not getting the real help he needed.

"I feel he made peace with God because he spent a lot of time in prayer and bible study near the end of his life. Yes, I would marry him again, but I would want a healthy way to share our lives together with our children. Hindsight you know. His good side was such a fine loving man with two personalities. I don't know how this happens, but it does"

Since this was an anonymous survey, I have no way of knowing who wrote this, but she appears to have some unresolved issues that are holding her back. Counseling may be needed to help her get on with her life.

Respondent # 4

The next respondent gave some interesting comments.

She indicated that her husband was unfaithful but not abusive. She said, "If my husband had been abusive, I would not have stayed married for 34 years. I do not tolerate abuse from anyone. In statement No. 4, you asked if I would marry him again. I said most likely because there was a 27 year difference in our ages and when I was growing up I did not have a father figure in my life. Statement number 3; was he unfaithful? Yes, he fathered a child by our baby sitter."

Respondent # 5

"I stayed in my marriage because of the children. As they say, it was my second marriage. The first marriage ended due to an unfaithful husband. I decided to stay in the second marriage to make it a perfect family, to show the first husband what he missed. Also, the second marriage gave me the best two sons that I could ask for and that gave the second husband a pass. I saved him a good job and he went down hill. We are now separated and the sons are grown and on their own. I would not change not having had my sons for anything, even a failed marriage."

Respondent # 6

"We wanted four children, two boys and two girls. God blessed us with that family. Although we had our usual ups and downs (minor), at no time did we ever think of ending our marriage. I was 'till death do us part, February 8, 2009. But I have faith we will meet again in heaven. We were best friends as well as mates, and I think communication was a key factor in the success of our marriage. Also commitment."

Respondent # 7

This respondent had some interesting comments. She said her husband was not abusive because she wouldn't let him, and to her knowledge, he had not been unfaithful.

She said, "I love my husband very much. That is why I stay. We have had some hard times, but we lean on God more." She also said that they were not each other's first choice.

Respondent #8

This respondent's husband was abusive and unfaithful. This is her statement. " I stayed married to him for 24 years. I lived with him 10 years. It was the most miserable years of my life. Fourteen years I've spent, realizing it wasn't my fault. It's like going into rehab, not knowing who you are and when the treatment is over you look in the mirror and say it's me. I'm back. I loved him, but thank God he's gone."

Respondent # 9

This respondent had a marriage that seemed to be ideal. "Having been married before with three children, marriage was not a high priority for me. When I met my husband, he was so good to my children and that won me over. We were a team. He was the preacher and I was the musician. We never had a fight. He was always kind to me as well as to my children; a great provider. We worked through many financial problems, health problems with me, namely breast cancer, with complete healing."

Respondent # 10

This respondent had a lot to say. She described two marriages. "I was married at age sixteen and forty three. We first met when I was 12. We had four children. He was abusive and unfaithful and still considers himself a ladies man. We still love each other and are friends to this day. He definitely was my first choice and I was his. He was not a good family caretaker. What he did, he did well. He was raised in the church and is still under the impression that he can get himself straight to go to church. I would not remarry him. Our love and admiration remain."

"My second husband took good care of me and my children. They were young adults. He died in 1992. He was not abusive; unfaithful, I do not know. I definitely enjoyed marriage the second time around."

"He was married seven times and was a good husband to them all. He was raised in the church and sang religious songs constantly; did not attend church on a regular basis. "

"I loved being married both times. I have been by myself for the last four years and have enjoyed the single life and not dating at this time in my life."

Respondent # 11

This is another long story. "We married while in college. We were young, immature and I had not experienced any time on my own. We had great times together."

"He was very much a provider, always doing for me. After five years of marriage, we started a family and had three children in six years. We both continued to work, and I feel that we gave less time to each other. We were not of the same religion and did not share the same values. He strayed two times that I know of, both times with secretaries much younger than him. They were different from me, looking for something outside of their own unhappy marriage. They gave him attention and excitement. We worked through both times, the second time more painful than the first. He was placing most of the blame on me. After counseling, I discovered it was his inability to face responsibility. I wanted to separate but did not want to divorce. I needed space from the pain.

"He did not want to separate and slowly gave up the affair. I continued to pray and ask for God's healing.

"He gave me the strength to get through the most difficult time of my life. I did not want to break our family apart and felt that I could sacrifice the pain for my children. I strongly believe in marriage vows, and I wanted to fulfill my promise to God, if I possibly could. We made it through difficult times, but it took a long time to heal. I grew a lot and my faith became stronger. And I became a different person because of the experience.

"Today we are happy and enjoy our life together. We treasure our family and we are both grateful that we did not give up on our marriage. Have I forgotten it? No. Have I forgiven? Yes. Do we still love each other? Yes, very much so."

Respondent # 12

"I stayed because I had two children for him. I did not want to take a chance with another man. My children loved their father. I did not want them to experience a bad stepfather like I did until he left her with her three by my father and his two. My mother was left with five children to feed and clothe in a small east Texas college town on a small salary. They sent money when they wanted to, not when it was needed weekly or bimonthly.

Respondent # 13

"I met my husband when I first came to Dallas for my first teaching job. I met him at church on a Wednesday night near the end of August. We saw each other every day and married in January. When talking of marriage, we both thought of it as a life time commitment. We married and have always been crazy about each other and have always enjoyed having fun. The most important part of our marriage has been focused on the church. In our 41 years of marriage, we have attended church at least three times a week. It has always come first. We have also had most of our friends at church. We have never drank or smoked. We have two children who are married and are raising their children in the same way. Our goal is to be happy now and in heaven. I also told my students that I was married to the sweetest man in the world. And I still think so. God is watching over me. I have been blessed."

Respondent # 14

"My husband and I had been married for over 38 years when he passed away from cancer. During that time our marriage was blessed with three wonderful children. I mentioned to a co-worker one day that it was my thirtieth anniversary. My co-worker replied that was long enough for 28 good years of marriage and he was about right.

My husband and I both laughed at that comment. Many times we discussed why it was that we were able to stay married when so many around us had not. Certainly love didn't keep us together all those years because there were times we were not as close as others. While we did love our kids greatly, I'm not sure that was enough to keep us committed to one another."

Respondent #15

"My husband and I are Mexicans. Our culture is very patriarchal, however, he agrees that men and women should be equal in a relationship. I think that this common issue helps us to have an open communication. We have only been married for a year. But I know that our relationship is strong and will last a good while. I made the best choice of my life."

Respondent #16

"My husband and I did not listen to other people, not even his or my family. We trusted each other, that we did not see, we tried to trust in each other. We did not let anyone tell us about the other, not even our family members. When one pick/select a marriage mate, you think about what you would do to make your marriage successful. We had our ups and downs but we never went to bed/sleep angry or mad at each other."

Respondent #17

"I was married for 52 years. My husband passed away. We had six daughters. The marriage was a very good marriage. Our marriage began at the age of two persons, 17 and 18. We worked together and had a home within five years. I now live with my fifth daughter. I live in, but we loved each other. I now have eight grandchildren and 10 great grandchildren. The marriage stayed because we were both willing to work for our marriage."

Respondent #18

"I never had a desire to marry, one reason being; looking at my parents marriage, I did not want any part of a male in my life acting like my father. And my sister's husband cheated on her and now she is big as three people and gambles all the time."

CHAPTER 17

The Never Ending Story

Today is November 30, 2009. I dreamed about Florence last night.

He was supposed to be dead, and we had wrapped him up and covered his head. Then I noticed that the cover was moving, I uncovered his head and sure enough, he was alive. I quickly ran to call my niece to tell her the good news. His face was dark and looked like a skeleton. It had no eyes and teeth. Today is December 2, 2009. I had another dream about Florence last night. This time I saw his face. He was lying in bed but he looked so happy and healthy. When I walked up to the bed, he looked at me and said, "What are we going to do"?

I had dreamed about him many times during the last year, but this was the first time I had seen his face clearly. When I told my friend, Catherine, about my dreams a few months ago, she told me that when you see your loved ones face clearly in your dream, they are telling you that everything is all right.

Today is December 3, 2009, the anniversary of my husband's death, I had to work in the afternoon, so I went to visit the grave during the morning hours. I had bought a small Christmas tree to put on his grave and some poinsettias. As I drove away, I could see them in the distance. I did not have a pity party. I guess I am approaching a level of acceptance. It is time for a new beginning.

Writing this story brings back so many memories, many that are very unpleasant. From this day forward, I will only concentrate on the good times and look on the bad times as a bad dream from which I have finally awakened. I wonder how many more years it will be until I am lying there beside him for all eternity. My name there on the headstone with his is a reality check. It says that one day I will be there beside him in the grave and our souls will be in heaven

As I look back over the years and remember the things he said and did to me, I can't believe I stayed with him. Even after he left me, I took him back. Was it love or stupidity? Whatever it was, knowing what I know now I would do it all over again.

After this book is completed and published, I would like to do a sequel, which would include a worldwide survey and get thousands of readers' responses.

This survey gives a brief glimpse into the issues of marriage.

CHAPTER 18

Parade of the Squirrels

It was February 7, 2010. It was Sunday morning, a very unlikely day for a parade. But of course the squirrels didn't know that. It was also our anniversary date. Had he lived, we would have been married for 55 years.

I got up early as I always do on a Sunday morning. I try to be on time for church because I play for the Sunday School and I also teach a Sunday school class. I did my scriptures and meditation and went to the kitchen to make coffee. Coffee is a ritual in itself.

After drinking my coffee, I made breakfast which consisted of a piece of bacon, a piece of dry toast and a banana. Sometimes I eat other fruit as well. After breakfast, I took my huge glass of water to the bedroom to take my medication. I call it my mini drug store. Yes, some of you reading this have mini drug stores, too.

I had planned to leave church and go by the grave site to visit my husband's grave, after all, this was our anniversary. I turned my hair curlers on and proceeded to take my shower.

When I got out of the shower, I looked at the clock and it said 9:00. My time was running out. I only had 30 minutes to finish dressing and get to church. I decided that I did not have time to curl my hair, so I grabbed one of my emergency wigs and carefully placed it on my head. By the way, I hate wigs with a passion, but sometimes they are necessary evils. I finished dressing and rushed out and got in my car. I live less than a mile from the church, so it only took a short time to get there.

When I arrived at the church, I noticed there were no cars on the parking lot. I thought that was a bit unusual because even though I always tried to be on time, there were people who always arrived before me. I decided to look at my watch and low and behold, I was an hour early, so I decided to go visit the grave site, since I had a whole hour to wait before church and the memorial park was only about five minutes away.

When I entered the memorial park, a squirrel ran across the road in front of the car. He ran as if he were moving to a marching band. What a sight to behold.

I continued my journey through the memorial park to the Garden of Gethsemane. I exited my car and made my way to the grave site. I did not have much to say. Somehow, the squirrel had left me dumbfounded, because it brought back so many memories: How he loved to hunt squirrels, how he loved to cook and eat squirrels or sit in our garage or on our patio and watch them play. I stood there at his grave for a while. All I said was, "Happy Anniversary. I love you ,bye-bye."

I returned to my car and while driving out of the park, another squirrel was running across in front of my car, still moving to the beat of the marching band. Then, just before I drove out of the park, I saw something that I had never seen before, a mobile or wind chime, hanging from a tree. My husband loved mobiles. He liked the noisy ones that would clatter when the wind blew.

I left the memorial park and arrived at church on time.

EPILOGUE

You have just finished reading my book. You read about the good, the bad and the ugly. Did the book live up your expectations? Were you bored to tears?

I do not want this book to be misleading. I am not advocating that women, regardless of the situation, should stay in a marriage. I would hasten to say that I strongly believe that women sometimes make decisions without thinking it through. Sometimes I think the decision is made because of pride or what other people say or think.

There was no one in my family or circle of friends who thought I should stay with my husband and after he left me they felt I should not let him come back. I wish I had felt the same way, but I did not.

I wanted him to come back, but I had too much pride to ask, but I told him if he ever wanted to come back, he would have to ask permission. The day he asked if he could come back was a happy day for me.

Writing this book has been healing for me. The letters we wrote to each other in the book are all a figment of my imagination, but they seem so real to me. It was as if I really wrote to him and he really wrote me back. If I feel the need to write more letters, I will. Of course, the letters will not be a part of this book. I will continue to go to the grave site and take flowers and talk to him from time to time. I may even have a pity party or two.

I don't know what the future holds for me, but one thing I do know. Love is something you can't automatically turn on or off. You cannot will yourself to love somebody and you cannot will yourself to stop.

I have to keep reminding myself that he is never coming back.

What will happen with Tiger Woods" marriage? Will his wife take him back. All I can say is that she should follow her heart. Don't let pride make the decision for you. Sometimes love is not enough.

I am adding a blank questionnaire to my book. Please fill it out and mail it back. If you wish to email the responses, my email address is minterdnt@aol.com.

I would also like to encourage family members and friends to pay attention to your loved ones. If you think they display behaviors that suggest they may be bipolar, depressed or be suffering from any illness that needs a doctor's attention, do all you can to try and get a proper diagnosis and treatment for the individual.

When I looked at the manifestations of bipolar illness, I realized that there are probably thousands and thousands of undiagnosed cases. You see so many people with maladaptive behavior. Among all of the illnesses it could be, I'm sure many of them are bipolar. We have quite a few school age children who have been diagnosed with bipolar disease.

This realization was brought to my attention this morning. I turned the television on in the breakfast nook and sat down to eat my breakfast. Very soon after I sat down, the news reporter announced that Marie Osmond's 18-year-old son was dead. He committed suicide. He left a note indicating that he was depressed. Did he have an illness that had gone undiagnosed? Was he in counseling? Had anyone noticed his depression?

I do not know the answer to any of these questions, but the tragedy reminds us that we need to pay more attention to our family members. If someone doesn't tell the doctor, he can't help us.

I continue to miss my husband and I guess I always will. I just live from day-to-day and try to let my family and friends know that I care about them.

I realize that I will finish this earthly journey without him, but that our bodies will be side by side for all eternity and our souls will be together in heaven for all eternity.

Every day I wish for "Just One More Night."

My Mother and me

Seeing and Remembering

Seeing and Remembering

To my husband, Florence

I see you in the morning light
And when the night is new
When I'm looking at the moon, I'm seeing you.
When the rain falls, I see you in every raindrop
When the wind blows, I feel your breath upon my face
When the thunder rolls, I hear your voice calling out to me
Saying
"All is well"
When I travel, I see you shopping for hats at every stop.
When the door opens, I hear you coming in, whistling
with your walking cane clicking and yelling,
"Did the bell ring yet?" I see you in my dreams
When I look out the back door, I see you plowing in the garden.
I see you mowing the lawn
I see you training the bird dogs,
Or just sitting on the patio or in the garage
Every where I go and in everything I do, I see you.
And when I see, I remember
I remember that for almost fifty four years, we were joined together as one.
I remember how we raised and cared for our family together.
I remember the good times and the bad times.
I remember our private time together
Precious memories, how they linger
How they ever flood my soul
How they linger, ever near me
Precious memories take control.
Florence, my life, my love, I remember you.
Goodbye for now.
See you in heaven

Your wife, Dorothy

Florence Gets General Motors
25-Year Service Award

It's Over There

Summer Vacation

On Tour - Amish Country

Graduation Day, 1985

At My Sister Viola's House California - 1972

Ready to Board Alaskan Cruise

Painting the Shed

In Deep Thought

2009 Dennis Stephen's Christmas Party

RELECTIONS

As I entered the house, I heard my phone beep- ing. It was a message from my publisher telling me that my book was ready for me to look at and do the final proof reading. I was really tired and told him I would come by the next morning and pick it up, and I did.

We talked about the book and what may need to be changed. He told me to bring it home, proofread it again and make any changes that were needed, be- cause the next time I brought it in, he would send it to the printers. He said he wanted me to read every word and make sure I did not overlook any mistakes, even though he would give it a final look.

I brought the manuscript home and began to read it. One thing I noticed was that only two incidents of infidelity occurred from 1955 to 1968. After 1968 no other incident occurred until 1977. That is the year the relationship began and lasted until about 1990. She ended it because she became afraid of him because of his bipolar illness.

Before the affair, I had only known her as a very nice person who was very dedicated to her family. Most of the abuse occurred during those years also. I guess those years were so traumatic that they over- shadowed the good years.

After he retired in 1993, we began to travel a lot, as long as he was able. I am not trying to justify and certainly not condone his behavior; just trying to get it into perspective. Everyone knows that one incident of abuse or infidelity is one too many, and for many couples, it ends their relationship.

I realize for the very first time that my good years of marriage far out weighed my bad years, and I'm glad we stayed together until his death separated us.

CPSIA information can be obtained
at www.ICGtesting.com
Printed in the USA
FSHW022339200319
56468FS

9 781643 672847